Optimal Business Strategy "Master the Art of strategies"

About Book

Optimal business strategies are complex to formulate and execute, especially in the face of potentially disruptive innovations and discontinuous change. This book will help you to recognise these changes in the competitive environment and respond with effective strategies and agile business models are fundamental to the success of modern organizations.

Dedication

I would like to express a special debt of gratitude to my wife Rajeshree and my two daughters Rupeshi & Kavya, Mr. ADS Arora and Mr. Praveen Mehta for their support and guidance would like to express a special debt of gratitude to my wife Rajeshree and my two daughters Rupeshi & Kavya

About the Author

Gajanan Shirke, a hotel consultant, has years of extensive experience in the hospitality industry. His thirst for learning and aspiration to become a multi-faceted expert in the hotel industry helped him rise from employment to becoming an independent professional in the hospitality sector. Since his last assignment as General Manager at Kamat Hotels, he has become a renowned hotel consultant with a proven track record of developing, training and growing some of the best-known hotels, restaurants and fast-food joints in the Indian market. He was appointed as an expert consultant for The Eighth meeting of the Board of Studies for Hotel Management & Catering Technology. He is a visiting faculty at various Hotel Management Colleges and has trained over a thousand hospitality professionals. He has completed numerous pre and post opening hotel consultancies in India and overseas. In order to spread his extensive knowledge to aspiring hotel professionals, Gajanan has penned a large number of books spanning different segments of the hospitality industry. Starting from his first book 'Bar Management and Operations published in 2010, he has written 59 books including Hospitality Management, Food and Beverage Management, Hotel Engineering Management, Front office Management, Hotel Housekeeping Management, The Cookery Trilogy advance Cookery Theory, The Cookery Trilogy, Foundation of Cookery, The Cookery Trilogy... The Basic Cookery Book, Hotel Sales and Marketing, Hospitality Industry accounting & fundamentals, Customer Interaction Excellence in Hospitality, History of Indian Cuisine volume 1, History of

Indian Cuisine volume 2, Hotel owner's Manual, Hotel Security & prevention, Training Manager0s Manual, Exceptional Service In Hospitality Six Sigma way, etc.

Chapter One: Economics for Managers

01.1. Fundamental Ideas

The significance or importance of business/managerial economics can be discussed as:

1. Business economics is concerned with those aspects of traditional economics which are relevant for business decision making in real life. These are adapted or modified with a view to enable the manager take better decisions. Thus, business economic accomplishes the objective of building a suitable tool kit from traditional economics.

2. It also incorporates useful ideas from other disciplines such as psychology, sociology, etc. If they are found relevant to decision making. In fact, business economics takes the help of other disciplines having a bearing on the business decisions in relation various explicit and implicit constraints subject to which resource allocation is to be optimized.

3. Business economics helps in reaching a variety of business decisions in a complicated environment.

Certain examples are:

(i) What products and services should be produced?
(ii) What input and production technique should be used?
(iii) How much output should be produced and at what prices it should be sold?
(iv) What are the best sizes and locations of new plants?
(v) When should equipment be replaced?
(vi) How should the available capital be allocated?

4. Business economics makes a manager a more competent model builder. It helps him appreciate the essential relationship characterizing a given situation.

5. at the level of the firm. Where its operations are conducted though known focus functional areas, such as finance, marketing, personnel and production, business economics serves as an integrating agent by coordinating the activities in these different areas.

6. Business economics takes cognizance of the interaction between the firm and society, and accomplishes the key role of an agent in achieving the social and economic welfare goals. It has come to be realized that a business, apart from its obligations to shareholders, has certain social obligations. Business economics focuses attention on these social obligations as constraints subject to which business decisions are taken. It serves as an instrument in furthering the economic welfare of the society through socially oriented business decisions.

Managerial Economics is a developing subject. The scope of managerial economics refers to its area of study. Managerial economics has its roots in economic theory. The empirical nature of managerial economics makes its scope wider. Managerial economics provides management with strategic planning tools that can be used to get a clear perspective of the way the business world works and what can be done to maintain profitability in an ever changing environment. Managerial economics refers to those aspects of economic theory and application which are directly relevant to the practice of management and the decision making process within the enterprise. Its scope does not extend to macroeconomic theory and the economics of public policy which will also be of interest to the manager. While considering the scope of managerial economics we have to understand whether it is positive economics or normative economics.

Positive versus Normative Economics:

Most of the managerial economists are of the opinion that managerial economics is fundamentally normative and prescriptive in nature. It is concerned with what decisions ought to be made. The application of managerial economics is inseparable from consideration of values or norms, for it is always concerned with the achievement of objectives or the optimization of goals. In managerial economics, we are interested in what should happen rather than what does happen. Instead of explaining what a firm is doing, we explain what it should do to make its decision effective.

I. **Positive Economics:** A positive science is concerned with 'what is'. Robbins regards economics as a pure science of what is, which is not concerned with moral or ethical questions. Economics is neutral between ends. The economist has no right to pass judgment on the wisdom or folly of the ends itself. He is simply concerned with the problem of resources in relation to the ends desired. The manufacture and sale of cigarettes and wine may be injurious to health and therefore morally unjustifiable, but the economist has no right to pass judgment on these since both satisfy human wants and involve economic activity.

II. **Normative Economics:** Normative economics is concerned with describing what should be the things. It is, therefore, also called prescriptive economics. What price for a product should be fixed, what wage should be paid, how income should be distributed and so on, fall within the purview of normative economics?

It should be noted that normative economics involves value judgments. Almost all the leading managerial economists are of the opinion that managerial economics is fundamentally normative and prescriptive in nature. It refers mostly to what ought to be and cannot be neutral about the ends. The application of managerial economics is inseparable from consideration of values, or norms for it is always concerned with the achievement of objectives or the optimization of goals.

Further, in managerial economics, we are interested in what should happen rather than what does happen. Instead of explaining what a firm is doing, we explain what it should do to make its decision effective. Managerial economists are generally preoccupied.

Demand Analysis and Forecasting

A firm is an economic organisation which transforms inputs into output that is to be sold in a market. Accurate estimation of demand, by analysing the forces acting on demand of the product produced by the firm, forms the vital issue in taking effective decision at the firm level. A major part of managerial decision making depends on accurate estimates of demand. When demand is estimated, the manager does not stop at the stage of assessing the current demand but estimates future demand as well. This is what is meant by demand forecasting. This forecast can also serve as a guide to management for maintaining or strengthening market position and enlarging profit. Demand analysis helps in identifying the various factors influencing the demand for a firm's product and thus provides guidelines to manipulate demand. The main topics covered are: Demand Determinants, Demand Distinctions and Demand Forecasting.

Cost and Production Analysis

Cost analysis is yet another function of managerial economics. In decision making, cost estimates are very essential. The factors causing variation in costs must be recognised and allowed for if management is to arrive at cost estimates which are significant for planning purposes. The determinants of estimating costs, the relationship between cost and output, the forecast of cost and profit are very vital to a firm. An element of cost uncertainty exists because all the factors determining costs are not always known or controllable. Managerial economics touches these aspects of cost analysis as an effective knowledge and the application of which is corner stone for the success of a firm.

Production analysis frequently proceeds in physical terms. Inputs play a vital role in the economics of production. The factors of production otherwise called inputs, may be combined in a particular way to yield the maximum output. Alternatively, when the price of inputs shoots up, a firm is forced to work out a combination of inputs so as to ensure that this combination becomes the least cost combination. The main topics covered under cost and production analysis are production function, least cost combination of factor inputs, factor productiveness, returns to scale, cost concepts and classification, costoutput relationship and linear programming.

Inventory Management

An inventory refers to a stock of raw materials which a firm keeps. Now the problem is how much of the inventory is the ideal stock. If it is high, capital is unproductively tied up. If the level of inventory is low, production will be affected. Therefore, managerial economics will use such methods as Economic Order Quantity (EOQ) approach, ABC analysis with a view to minimising the inventory cost. It also goes deeper into such aspects as motives of holding inventory, cost of holding inventory, inventory control, and main methods of inventory control and management.

Advertising

To produce a commodity is one thing and to market it is another. Yet the message about the product should reach the consumer before he thinks of buying it. Therefore, advertising forms an integral part of decision making and forward planning. Expenditure on advertising and related types of promotional activities is called selling costs by economists. There are different methods for setting advertising budget: Percentage of Sales Approach, All You can Afford Approach, Competitive Parity Approach, Objective and Task Approach and Return on Investment Approach.

Pricing Decision, Policies and Practices

Pricing is very important area of managerial economics. The control functions of an enterprise are not only productions but pricing as well. When pricing a commodity, the cost of production has to be taken into account. Business decisions are greatly influenced by pervading market structure and the structure of markets that has been evolved by the nature of competition existing in the market. Pricing is actually guided by consideration of cost plan pricing and the policies of public enterprises. The knowledge of the pricing of a product under conditions of oligopoly is also essential. The price system guides the manager to take valid and profitable decision.

Profit Management

A business firm is an organisation designed to make profits. Profits are acid test of the individual firm's performance. In appraising a company, we must first understand how profit arises. The concept of profit maximisation is very useful in selecting the alternatives in making a decision at the firm level. Profit forecasting is an essential function of any management. It relates to projection of future earnings and involves the analysis of actual and expected behaviour of firms, the sales volume, prices and competitor's strategies, etc. The main aspects covered under this area are the nature and measurement of profit, and profit policies of special significance to managerial decision making. Managerial economics tries to find out the cause and effect relationship by factual study and logical reasoning. For example, the statement that profits are at a maximum when marginal revenue is equal to marginal cost, a substantial part of economic analysis of this deductive proposition attempts to reach specific conclusions about what should be done. The logic of linear programming is deduction of mathematical form. In fine, managerial economics is a branch of normative economics that draws from descriptive economics and from well established deductive patterns of logic.

Capital Management

Planning and control of capital expenditures is the basic executive function. The managerial problem of planning and control of capital is examined from an economic stand point. The capital budgeting process takes different forms in different industries. It involves the equi-marginal principle. The objective is to assure the most profitable use of funds, which means that funds must not be applied when the managerial returns are less than in other uses. The main topics dealt with are: Cost of Capital, Rate of Return and Selection of Projects. Thus we see that a firm has uncertainties to rock on with. Therefore, we can conclude that the subject matter of managerial economics consists of applying economic principles and concepts towards adjusting with these uncertainties of the firm. In recent years, there is a trend towards integration of managerial economics and Operation Research. Hence, techniques such as linear Programming, Inventory Models, Waiting Line Models, Bidding Models, Theory of Games, etc. have also come to be regarded as part of managerial economics.

Identify your customers' maximum willingness to pay and the forces that shape it

The first lesson centers on the customer demand for products and services. What do customers need, how many units do they want, and how much are they willing to pay for it? Suppose that a customer's maximum willingness to pay for a single unit of a product is denoted by B, a number. What every manager wants to know is the value of B. Economics demonstrates how to organize one's thinking on when, why and how much B changes.

The manager's task is to get as precise an estimate as possible of B. A number of competing methods and models are used to estimate B. Some methods attempt to estimate consumers' stated preferences through the use of surveys, while other methods attempt to estimate consumers' revealed preferences through the use of market data and/or controlled experiments. Expert judgment is sometimes used to interpret survey data. And sometimes, analytical models (such as conjoint analysis and discrete choice models) are used to estimate the value of the attributes of the product.

B is altered by many forces. Economics courses tend to emphasize the market/industry/economy wide forces such as changes in customer tastes, shifting income and expenditure considerations and changes in the prices of competing and complementary products. However, many of the forces that shift B are company specific and within its control. Companies often emphasize the functional, emotional and life-changing attributes of their products and service in their advertising and communication campaigns.

For instance, Peloton, the exercise equipment and media-company, emphasizes the life-transforming experience of joining the community of (remote) bicycling aficionados. Amazon emphasizes the functional and transformational experience of Amazon Prime because of the convenience of free two-day delivery of products, and on-demand access to movies, TV, music and books. And the advertising campaign slogan for the first Apple iPhone, "This changes everything" refers to the functional, emotional and life-changing aspects of owning an iPhone.

Managers must also grapple with the question of how best to sell their products and services. Should products and services be sold via an auction (as on eBay) or with posted prices (take it or leave it) or should they be sold via negotiation? Auctions are better when B is widely dispersed which is why auctions are used to sell art, wine and rarely traded products. However, auctions require an investment of time - a luxury in the 21st century economy. Posted prices have become the dominant method of selling standardized products because buyers look for immediate gratification. And negotiation is the preferred mode of selling when products and services must be customized and when there is heterogeneity amongst customers.

Know your economic costs, C

For economists, all costs are opportunity costs. Rather than focus only on the direct cost of an activity in the way that accounting does, economists ask, "what must the firm give up to engage in this activity?" Framed this way, lost benefits also count as costs. The fact that a company own assets- such as an office building- does not mean that its cost of ownership are zero. The cost of using an office building includes, in addition to the direct costs of operating the building, the lost rent from leasing it.

In fact, the most significant costs that companies incur do not show up on their income statements. Many companies raise equity capital from investors. On an income statement, the cost of equity is assumed to equal zero since there is no explicit payment that the company must make to investors. However, equity investors do expect a financial return. In fact, if they do not receive an adequate return, they will likely put their money elsewhere. By forcing companies to acknowledge that equity capital carries an implicit cost, economics forces the company to raise the bar on investments that it chooses.

If ignoring implicit costs is an error of omission, counting costs that have been incurred and that cannot be recouped, is an error of commission. This is known as the sunk cost fallacy. The most famous instance of sunk costs distorting decisions is when the British and French governments, after jointly launching the Concorde supersonic passenger airline in 1976, chose to continue investing in the project despite mounting evidence that its economic prospects were not promising. The original budget for the Concorde was 70m. The eventual cost was 1.3b.

One reason why managers fall victim to the sunk cost fallacy is that they are unwilling to accept that their prior investments have failed. Managers often tell themselves that success requires patience and determination. As well as incremental investments! The behavioral economists, Daniel Kahneman and Amos Tversky, proposed an explanation for why people and firms are willing to throw good money after bad. They call it loss aversion- the idea that people prefer to avoid a loss compared to a gain of an equivalent sum. In the corporate world, it is not uncommon for managers to take on more risk so that the company has a shot at salvaging its prior investments, rather than acknowledge losses.

Create Economic Value (EV)

EV = B – C. **Figure 1** shows that the wider the wedge between B and C, the greater is the economic value created. If a firm cannot create EV, either because it cannot boost B or because it cannot keep C lower than B, the signals are clear - the firm should contemplate exit.

Figure 1

B_0

C_0

The task for a manager is to figure out how to create EV. Should the manager spend more money upgrading products, or on advertising campaigns, or on modernizing infrastructure? Or should the manager reduce costs by outsourcing production or by altering its product and input mix?

In **Figure 2**, widening the gap between B and C requires the firm to increase C. Increasing C by 50,000 leads to a 100,000 increase in B. Generally speaking, it is difficult to increase B without increasing C (unless there are many inefficiencies that can be reduced or eliminated). The luxury hotel chain, A, must spend a lot to improve and maintain its facilities and service because it caters to a high B customer. In contrast, the budget hotel chain, B can incur a small C because its customers have a low B.

Figure 2

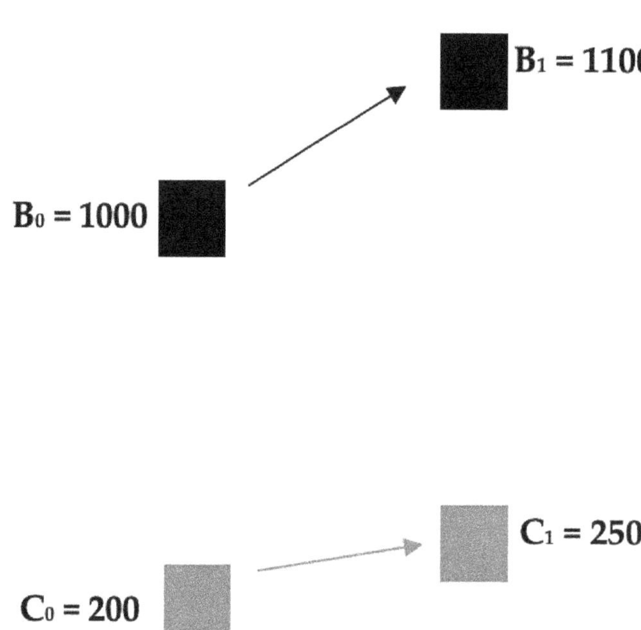

Beware across the board reductions in C. Some components of C can be reduced without consequence for B. But reducing other components of C can be self-defeating. As **Figure 3** shows, reducing C by 50,000 leads to a 100,000 reduction in B.

Figure 3

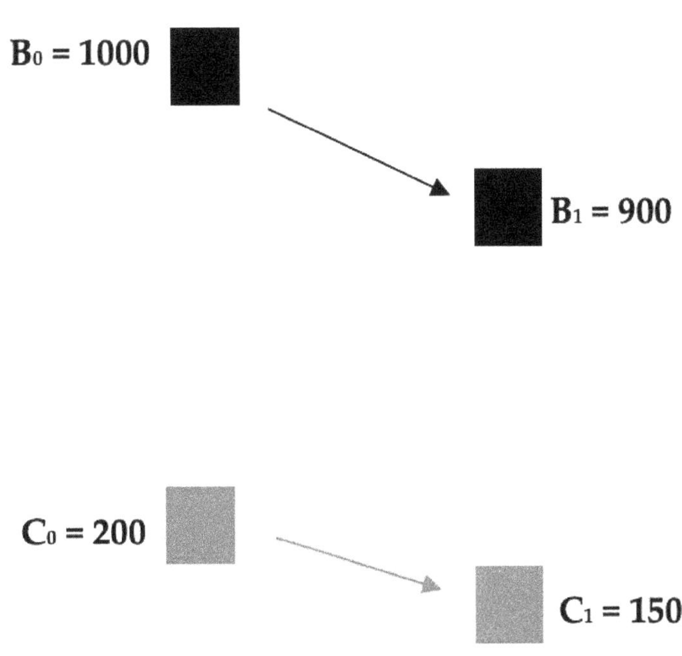

Of course, there is more than one B because people differ in their tastes, incomes and potential choices. Comparisons of EV across customers force managers to narrow the range of target customers. Some target customers may have a higher B than other target customers but may also force the firm to incur high C. Other target customers may require low C but command a small B. For every firm, the potential to create economic value is greater with some customers than with others. In fact, some customers are best avoided. The manager's task is to find those customers whose wants, needs and B best match with the firm's offerings and capabilities.

Analyze the other players in your market

Every company's Value Net - the value created by a company's network- is influenced by 4 distinct sets of players: customers, suppliers, substitutors and complementors. Each set of players cooperates to increase EV but also competes to capture a greater share of EV.

Figure 4 is a reproduction of the Brandenburger-Nalebuff Value Net map. On the vertical dimension are the players your firm transacts with. Your suppliers provide raw materials, finished goods, labor, services and more. Your customers purchase your finished products, services and more.

Figure 4

The Value Net

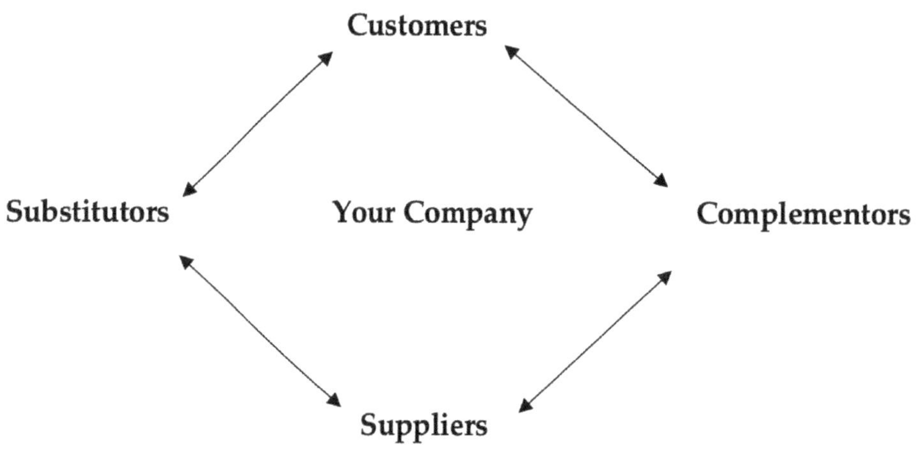

Customers

Substitutors **Your Company** **Complementors**

Suppliers

On the horizontal dimension are the players you interact, but do not, transact, with. Your substitutors are more than just your closest competitors. They also include those firms whose products are not as closely substitutable but never-the-less command the attention of your customers. For instance, American Airlines is a close substitutor for United Airlines. But Amtrak and the Megabus are also substitutors for United Airlines since your customers may consider trains and buses as alternatives to plane travel. Your complementors are those whose products and services are used with your products and services. They make your products (more) effective. For example, the Apple iPhone has hundreds of apps that are developed by independent firms and that are designed to integrate with the iPhone ecosystem.

Your task is to understand the interdependency among and between the sets of players- to understand your vulnerabilities and strengths as well as those of others. It is a mistake to think that all players' interests are opposed to yours at all times. Even substitutors, sometimes characterized as the enemy in business narratives, have interests that align with yours. For instance, Hyatt and Marriott have a common interest in seeing a growth in tourism and business travel even as they compete for the customers' business.

In assessing players, managers should examine their capabilities and intent. Some players may have burning ambitions but lack the capability to execute. Others may have capabilities but lack the vision. It is the task of the manager to discover the pathways- the formal and informal partnerships with players in the Value Net- that offer the most promising avenues for EV creation.

Prices depend on competition and bargaining

How prices are determined is one of the central lessons of economics. A discussion of competing models of price determination, such as perfect competition, monopoly and oligopoly, often account for between a third and a half of the time spent on lectures during a term. A general lesson from these models is that the (equilibrium) price for a product depends on the intensity of competition between companies, buyers and suppliers as well as the relative bargaining power of buyers, sellers, and suppliers.

Two examples illustrate this lesson. Suppose (as in **Figure 5**) that two firms are competing to sell a project to one consumer. The customer has a willingness to pay of 1m for the project. And suppose that it costs each firm 200,000 to deliver the project. Where are prices likely to settle?

Figure 5

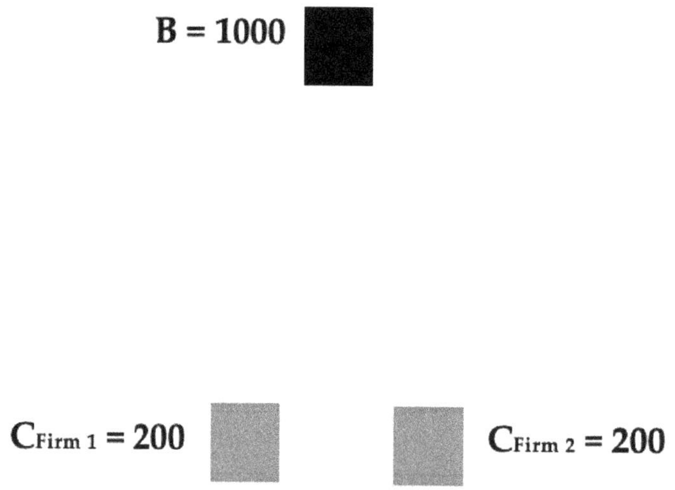

B = 1000

$C_{Firm\ 1}$ = 200

$C_{Firm\ 2}$ = 200

To answer this question, it is useful to compute each player's added value (AV). This is the difference between EV when that player exists and EV without that player. The buyer's AV equals 800,000 because EV with the buyer is 800,000 and EV without the buyer is 0. The AVs for either firm equal 0 because the absence of either firm makes no difference to EV. Consequently, it is assured that competition between the firms will push the price, P, to 200,000.

What if the firm's costs are not equal? Suppose, as in **Figure 6**, that two firms, Firm 1 and Firm 2 are competing with firm 1 incurring a cost of C1 = 200,000 and firm 2 incurring a cost, C2, = 250,000. B remains at 1m. The AV of the buyer is still 800,000. The AV of firm 1 is 50,000, its cost advantage versus firm 2, while the AV of firm 2 equals 0. Firm 1 will win the project because it can afford to undercut firm 2. The equilibrium price can fall anywhere between 200,000 and 250,000 and depends on the bargaining skills of the buyer and firm 1.

Figure 6

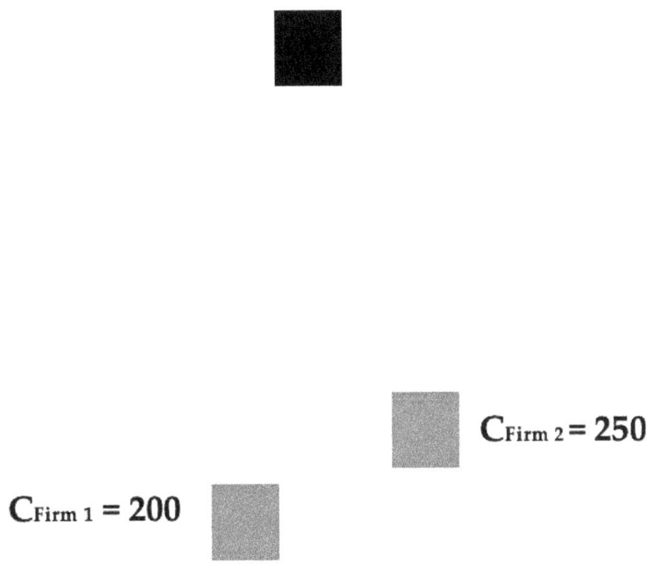

$C_{Firm\ 2} = 250$

$C_{Firm\ 1} = 200$

Your task is to create and capture economic value

EV can be rewritten as follows: B – C = (B – P) + (P – C). The term, B – P, is called consumer surplus (CS), the difference between the customer's maximum willingness to pay and the price paid. And the second term, P – C, is profit (P) margin. Hence, EV = CS + P.

The creation of economic value is only one element of the manager's mission. The other element is to capture it. Competing with other substitutors through prices, product differentiation and services, and bargaining with others, is one way for a firm to capture a bigger share of EV. The more effective way is to leverage the strengths of your complementors. Google's Nest started as a digital thermostat and alarm that allows people to control temperature inside the home and monitor security. By creating the Work with Google Assistant ecosystem, Google has allowed hundreds of complementors to co-create EV by linking with Google Assistant.

The firms that earn the biggest economic profits and the biggest economic losses are often in the news. The financial consulting firm, Stearn Stewart & Co. popularized the concept of economic value added (a proxy for economic profits) by publishing an annual list of the top wealth creators and wealth destroyers. In 2018, the leading wealth creator was Apple with an economic value added of 21.58b while the leading wealth destroyer was General Electric (GE) with an economic value added of - 20.544b.

General Electric's decline from one of the world's best managed companies to middling status has been staggering. Between 2015 and 2019, GE's combined economic value added was -77.84 billion. By Dec 30, 2019, its market capitalization had fallen to 104.64 billion- a decline of more than 136 billion in five years and a decline of more than 320 billion since 2007! Its bonds, rated AAA in 2001, are now BBB+, three notches above junk. And for the first time in more than a century, GE is no longer included on the Dow Jones Industrial Average.

What went wrong? In his analysis of GE and its CEO, Jeffrey Immelt, Geoffrey Colvin attributes the company's decline to poor capital allocation decisions. Under Immelt's tenure, GE spent more than 100 billion on acquisitions and 93 billion in stock buybacks. Between 2010 and 2014, when oil prices were high, GE acquired more than 9 businesses in the oil and gas sector paying top dollar. GE's 2015 bet on fossil fuels via its 10.6 billion purchase of Alstom was poorly timed since the tide had turned in favor of renewables. Immelt's worst capital allocation decision was to overleverage GE Capital by more than 250 billion. GE Capital began taking equity positions in commercial real estate- a bet that went south during the 2007 crisis.

It takes the passage of time to appreciate three profound principles at the heart of economics. The first is that the merit of any potential decision must begin with a balancing of the benefits and costs of the decision. The second is that decision-making requires marginal analysis, a comparison of the incremental benefits and costs for small changes from the status quo. And the third is that decision-making requires equilibrium thinking, a consideration of how other rational actors- buyers, suppliers, substitutors, complementors and others - respond to changes.

TYPES OF ECONOMIES OF SCALE

1. Internal Economies of Scale: 'Internal economies of scale' are the advantages enjoyed within the production unit. These economies are enjoyed by a single firm independently of the action of the other firms. For instance, one firm may enjoy the advantage of good management; another may have the advantage of more up-to-date machinery. Kinds of internal economies

1. Technical Economies: As the size of the firm is large, the availability of capital is more. Due to this, a firm can introduce up- to-date technologies; thereby the increase in the productivity

becomes possible. It is also possible to conduct research and development which will help to increase the quality of the product.

2. Financial Economies: It is possible for big firms to float shares in the market for capital formation. Small firms have to borrow capital whereas large firms can buy capital.

3. Managerial Economies: Division of labour is the result of large scale production. Right person can be employed in the right department only if there is division of labour. This will help a manager to fix responsibility to each department and thereby the productivity can be increased and the total production can be maximized.

4. Labour Economies: Large Scale production paves the way for division of labour. This is also known as specialization of labour. The specialization will increase the quality and ability of the labour. As a result, the productivity of the firm increases.

5. Marketing Economies: In production, the first buyer is the producer who buys the raw materials. As the size is large, the quantity bought is larger. This gives the producer a better bargaining power. Also he can enjoy credit facilities. All these are possible because of large scale production. Buying is the first function in marketing.

6. Economies of survival: A large firm can have many products. Even if one product fails in the market, the loss incurred in that product can be managed by the profit earned from the other products.

External economies of scale:

When many firms expand in a particular area – i.e., when the industry grows – they enjoy a number of advantages which are known as external economies of scale. This is not the advantage enjoyed by a single firm but by all the firms in the industry due to the structural growth. They are a) increased transport facilities b) Banking facilities c) Development of townships d) Information and communication development All these facilities are available to all firms in an industrial region.

DISECONOMIES OF SCALE

The diseconomies of the scale are a disadvantage to a firm or an industry or an organization. This necessarily increases the cost of production of a commodity or service. Further it delays the speed of the supply of the product to the market. These diseconomies are of two types:

a) Internal Diseconomies of Scale: and b) External Diseconomies of Scale

a. Internal Diseconomies of Scale: If a firm continues to grow and expand beyond the optimum capacity, the economies of scale disappear and diseconomies will start operating. For instance, if the size of a firm increases, after a point the difficulty of management arises to that particular firm which will increase the average cost of production of that firm. This is known as internal diseconomies of scale.

b. External Diseconomies of Scale: The term "External diseconomies of scale" refers to the threat or disturbance to a firm or an industry from factor lying outside it. For example a bus strike prevents the easy and correct entry of the workers into a firm. Similarly the rent of a firm increases very much if new economic units are established in the locality.

COST ANALYSIS

Cost refers to the total expenses incurred in the production of a commodity. The functional relationship between cost and output is expressed as 'Cost Function'. A Cost Function may be written as C = f (Q) where, C=Cost and Q=Quantity of output.

The determinants of cost of production are: the size of plant, the level of production, the nature of technology used, the quantity of inputs used, managerial and labour efficiency.

Cost Concepts and Classification 1. Money Cost 2. Real Cost 3. Explicit Cost 4. Implicit Cost 5. Economic Cost 6. Social Cost 7. Opportunity Cost 8. Sunk Cost 9. Floating Cost 10. Prime Cost 11. Fixed Cost 12. Variable Cost

1. Money Cost : Money cost or nominal cost is the total money expenses incurred by a firm in producing a commodity. It includes: cost of raw materials, payment of wages and salaries, payment of rent, interest on capital, expenses on fuel and power, expenses on transportation and so on.

2. Real Cost : Real cost is a subjective concept. Real cost refers to the payment made to compensate the efforts and sacrifices of all factor owners for their services in production. It includes the efforts and sacrifices of landlords in the use of land, capitalists to save and invest, and workers in foregoing leisure.

3. Explicit Cost : Explicit costs are the payments made by the entrepreneur to the suppliers of various productive factors. Explicit cost includes, wages, payment for raw material, rent for the building, interest for capital invested, expenditure on transport and advertisement, other expenses like license fee, depreciation and insurance charges, etc. It is also called Accounting Cost or Out of Pocket Cost or Money Cost.

4. Implicit Cost : The money rewards for the own services of the entrepreneur and the factors owned by himself and employed in production are known as implicit costs or imputed Costs.

5. Economic Cost: It refers to all payments made to the resources owned and purchased or hired by the firm in order to ensure their regular supply to the process of production. Economic Cost = Implicit Cost + Explicit Cost

6. Social Cost: It refers to the total cost borne by the society due to the production of a commodity. Social Cost is the cost that is not borne by the firm, but incurred by others in the society. For example, large business firms cause air pollution, water pollution and other damages in a particular area which involve cost to the society. It is also called as External Cost.

7. Opportunity Cost : It refers to the cost of next best alternative use. In other words, it is the value of the next best alternative foregone. For example, a farmer can cultivate both paddy and sugarcane in a farm land. If he cultivates paddy, the opportunity cost of paddy output is the amount of sugarcane output given up. Opportunity Cost is also called as 'Alternative Cost' or 'Transfer Cost'.

8. Sunk Cost : A cost incurred in the past and cannot be recovered in future is called as Sunk Cost. Sunk cost are unalterable, unrecoverable, and if once invested it should be treated as drowned. For example, if a firm purchases a specialized equipment designed for a special plant, the expenditure on this equipment is a sunk cost, because it has no alternative use Sunk cost is also called as 'Retrospective Cost'.

9. Floating Cost: It refers to all expenses that are directly associated with business activities but not with asset creation. It does not include the purchase of raw material as it is part of current assets. It includes payments like wages to workers, transportation charges, fee for power and administration. Floating cost is necessary to run the day-to-day business of a firm.

10. Prime Cost: All costs that vary with output, together with the cost of administration are known as Prime Cost. In short, Prime cost = Variable costs + Costs of Administration.

11. Fixed Cost : Fixed Cost does not change with the change in the quantity of output. In other words, expenses on fixed factors are called as fixed cost. For example, rent of the factory, watchman's wages, permanent worker's salary, payments for minimum equipments and machines insurance premium, deposit for power, license fee, etc fixed cost is also called as 'Supplementary Cost' or 'Overhead Cost'.

12. Variable Cost : These costs vary with the level of output. In other words, the costs incurred on variable factors are called variable costs. Examples of variable costs are: wages of temporary

workers, cost of raw materials, fuel cost, electricity charges, etc. Variable cost is also called as Prime Cost, Special Cost, or Direct Cost.

1.2. Demand

Demand Demand is the quantity of good and services that customers are willing and able to purchase during a specified period under a given set of economic conditions. The period here could be an hour, a day, a month, or a year. The conditions to be considered include the price of good, consumer's income, the price of the related goods, consumer's preferences, advertising expenditures and so on. The amount of the product that the customers are willing to buy, or the demand, depends on these factors. There are two types of demand. The first of these is called **direct demand**. This model of demand analysis individual demand for goods and services that directly satisfy consumers desires. The prime determinant of direct demand is the utility gained by consumption of goods and services. Consumers budget, product characteristics, individuals preferences are all important determinants of direct demand. The other type of demand is called **derived demand**. Derived demand is the demand resulting from the need to provide the final goods and services to the consumers. Intermediate goods, office machines are examples of derived demand. An other good example is mortgage credit. Mortgage credit demand is not demanded directly, but derived from the demand for housing.

Market demand function The market demand function for a product is a function showing the relation between the quantity demanded and the factors affecting the quantity of demand. A demand function for the good X can be expressed as follows: Quantity of product X demanded = Qx = f (the price of X, prices of related goods, expectations of price changes, income, preferences, advertising expenditures and so on.) For use in managerial decision making, the relation between quantity of demand and each demand determining variable must be specified.

Demand Curve The demand function specifies the relation between the quantity demanded and all factors that determine demand. But the demand curve expresses the relation between the price of a product and the quantity demanded, holding constant all the other factors affecting demand.

The Law of Demand

Demand refers to the willingness and ability of consumers to purchase a particular good or service at a specific price. In other words, it represents the quantity of a product or service that consumers are willing and able to buy at a particular price.

The law of demand is a fundamental concept in economics that states that, other things being equal, the quantity demanded of a good or service will decrease as its price increases, and vice versa. In other words, as the price of a good or service increases, people will be less likely to buy it and will instead look for substitutes. Conversely, as the price of a good or service decreases, people will be more likely to buy it.

This relationship between price and demand is typically represented graphically as a downward-sloping demand curve. The law of demand provides a basic understanding of how changes in price can affect the quantity of a good or service that consumers are willing to purchase. It is a cornerstone of microeconomic theory and is used to inform a wide range of business decisions, including pricing strategy, production planning, and market entry.

It's worth noting that while the law of demand is a robust and widely accepted principle, there are exceptions and qualifications. For example, certain goods, such as luxury items or necessities, may be less affected by changes in price. Additionally, the relationship between price and demand may be influenced by a wide range of factors, such as consumer income, preferences, and availability of substitutes.

Demand Curve and Demand Schedule

A demand curve is a graphical representation of the relationship between the price of a good or service and the quantity of that good or service that consumers are willing and able to purchase. The demand curve slopes downward from left to right, reflecting the law of demand, which states that, other things being equal, the quantity demanded of a good or service will decrease as its price increases.

A demand schedule, on the other hand, is a table that lists the various quantities of a good or service that consumers are willing and able to purchase at different prices. The demand schedule is used to calculate the demand curve by plotting the quantity demanded against the corresponding price for each price-quantity combination.

The demand curve and demand schedule provide valuable information to firms about how changes in price will affect the quantity of their product that consumers are willing to purchase. This information can be used to inform a wide range of business decisions, including pricing strategy, production planning, and market entry.

For example, a firm may use the demand curve to determine the price that will maximize its profits. By comparing the quantity demanded at different prices, the firm can identify the price at which the quantity demanded is highest, and thus the price that will generate the most revenue. The demand schedule can also be used to analyze how changes in consumer income or preferences, or the availability of substitutes, might affect the demand for a product.

Market Equilibrium

The point where supply and demand curves intersect represents the market clearing or market equilibrium price. An increase in demand shifts the demand curve to the right. The two curves then intersect at a higher price, which means consumers are willing to pay more for the product. Equilibrium prices typically change for most goods and services because factors affecting supply and demand are always changing. Free, competitive markets tend to push prices toward market equilibrium.

Market Demand vs. Aggregate Demand

The market for each good in an economy faces a different set of circumstances, which vary in type and degree. In macroeconomics, we also look at aggregate demand in an economy. Aggregate demand refers to the total demand by all consumers for all goods and services in an economy across all the markets for individual goods. Since aggregate demand includes all goods in an economy, it is not sensitive to competition or the substitution of goods. Nor is it due to changes in consumer preferences between various goods. Demand in individual goods markets can be affected by these factors.

Macroeconomic Policy and Demand

Fiscal and monetary authorities, such as the Federal Reserve, devote much of their macroeconomic policy-making to managing aggregate demand. If the Fed wants to reduce demand, it can raise interest rates and increase prices by curtailing the growth of the money supply and credit. If it needs to increase demand, the Fed can lower interest rates and increase the money supply, giving consumers and businesses more money to spend. In certain cases, even the Fed can't fuel demand. When unemployment is on the rise, people may not be able to afford to spend or take on cheaper debt, even with low interest rates.

The Bottom Line

Demand is a core economic concept that shows how much of a good or service consumers are willing to buy at different prices. The concept is used by businesses to determine prices and used by consumers to know when to make a purchase. The demand curve visually depicts how demand changes in relation to price: when price increases, demand decreases; when price decreases, demand increases.

1.3. Supply

The law of supply is a microeconomic law. It states that, all other factors being equal, as the price of a good or service increases, the quantity of that good or service that suppliers offer will increase, and vice versa. In plain terms, this law means that as the price of an item goes up, suppliers will attempt to maximize their profits by increasing the number of that item that they sell.

The following are the types of supply:

Market supply: It is the total amount of a good/ service that producers are capable or willing to deliver over a given time period. Suppose, in a market, there are many cashmere sellers. One may be able to supply it during a particular season. Others may be short of it for the time being. Another seller is getting the stock next week. The summation of these individual supply curves will constitute the market supply curve.

Short-Run Supply: The current supply is based on the organization's capital expenditure on fixed assets. To fulfill the supply, firms must adjust their fixed costs to a level that will minimize the average total cost of production. The organization will shut down production when the market price goes lower than the minimum average variable of the cost of that product.

Long Run Supply: It refers to the supply of goods when every input is variable. In the long run, organization will only be able to earn ordinary profit, hence there will be zero economic profit. This allows new firms to enter if they see positive economic profits, and older firms will exit the market if they face losses. This entry and exit average will keep the number of firms consistent in the market.

Factors Impacting Supply

Product Prices: As shown in the supply curve, when the price of a commodity increase, its supply increases as well. Vice-versa, supply will decrease automatically when the price of the commodity goes down. This is also understandable since most businesses manufacture products to earn profit and hence, higher prices motivate them to increase the supply.

Availability of Raw Material: Suppose a restaurant is popular for its onion rings. However, the market is short of onions due to the destruction of the crops. Due to this, the supply of onion rings will also go down. The supply will automatically go down if the raw material required to produce the product is insufficient. If there is sufficient raw material, then the supply will continue.

Producer's Expectations: If the product manufacturer believes that the prices of his products will increase in the foreseeable future, then he will increase production to ensure supply.

Similarly, if the producer anticipates a decline in the prices and demand of a product, they will cut short the supply of the product.

Costs of Input: Suppose the prices of one or more materials used in a product have increased. This will force the producer to plan out the supply of that product. In the worst-case scenario, the producer might decide to stop the supply of that product.

Supply Analysis

Supply refers to the quantity of a good or service that a firm or an industry is willing and able to produce and sell at various prices over a certain period of time. The supply of a good or service is determined by several factors, including production costs, technology, input prices, and the availability of factors of production.

The law of supply states that, other things being equal, an increase in price leads to an increase in the quantity supplied, and a decrease in price leads to a decrease in the quantity supplied. This relationship is based on the behavior of firms and the incentives they face. When the price of a good increases, firms have an incentive to produce and sell more of that good, as they can earn higher profits. Conversely, when the price of a good decreases, firms have less of an incentive to produce and sell that good, as their profits decline.

The law of supply is a basic principle of economics and is represented graphically by a supply curve, which shows the relationship between the price of a good and the quantity of the good that a firm is willing and able to produce and sell. The slope of the supply curve is upward, which means that as the price of a good increases, the quantity supplied of that good also increases. The law of supply is an important concept in both microeconomics and macroeconomics, and helps to explain how market prices are determined and how they respond to changes in market conditions.

Supply Curve and Supply Schedule

A supply curve is a graphical representation of the relationship between the price of a good or service and the quantity of that good or service that a firm or an industry is willing and able to produce and sell over a certain period of time. The supply curve slopes upward, which means that as the price of a good or service increases, the quantity supplied of that good or service also increases. This relationship is based on the law of supply, which states that, other things being equal, an increase in price leads to an increase in the quantity supplied, and a decrease in price leads to a decrease in the quantity supplied.

A supply schedule is a table that lists the prices of a good or service and the corresponding quantity supplied at each price. The supply schedule is a tabular representation of the information contained in the supply curve. It shows the same relationship between price and quantity supplied as the supply curve, but presents the information in a different format. The supply schedule is useful for analyzing the behavior of firms and the impact of changes in the market environment on the quantity supplied of a good or service.

Both the supply curve and supply schedule are important tools for analyzing the behavior of firms and the market conditions that influence the supply of goods and services. They help to illustrate the relationship between price and quantity supplied, and to demonstrate how changes in market conditions impact the supply of goods and services. By analyzing these relationships, firms and policymakers can make informed decisions and develop effective policies to support economic growth and development.

The resulting supply curve will slope upward, which means that as the price per apple increases, the quantity supplied of apples also increases. This relationship is consistent with the law of supply, which states that, other things being equal, an increase in price leads to an increase in the quantity supplied, and a decrease in price leads to a decrease in the quantity supplied.

1.4. Profit Maximization and Pricing

Profit maximization is a process business firms undergo to ensure the best output and price levels are achieved in order to maximise its returns. Influential factors such as sale price, production cost and output levels are adjusted by the firm as a way of realizing its profit goals. In business, profit maximization is a good thing, but it can be a bad thing for the client if, for example, lower-quality materials and labor are used or if the business decides to raise the prices for executing projects, all in pursuit of profit maximization.

Profit maximization is the act of achieving the highest revenue or profit. The sales level where profits are highest is at the strategic level. It is typically used as a benchmark for the best situation and for planning purposes. Profit maximization is simply, using a product in order to generate a desired profit or return on investment. Profit maximization can be achieved in a variety of ways, but usually requires a high level of specialization and knowledge because minimizing costs and maximizing revenues are two key concepts that must be addressed for this to occur. The most common benchmark for profit maximization is called breakeven point, which means that if a company can increase sales above this point, then they will not just maximize profits but also create an opportunity to grow in the future.

Profit Maximization Model

Profit Maximization model helps to predict the price-output behavior of a firm under changing market conditions like tax rates, wages and salaries, bonus, the degree of availability of resources, technology, fashions, tastes and preferences of consumers etc. It is a very simple and unambiguous model. It is the single most ideal model that can explain the normal behavior of a firm. It is often argued that no other alternative hypothesis can explain and predict the behavior of business firms better than **profit-maximization hypothesis**. This model gives a proper insight in to the working behavior of a firm. There are well developed mathematical models to explain this hypothesis in a systematic and scientific manner.

Profit-maximization implies earning highest possible amount of profits during a given period of time. A firm has to generate largest amount of profits by building optimum productive capacity both in the short run and long run depending upon various internal and external factors and forces. There should be proper balance between short run and long run objectives. In the short run a firm is able to make only slight or minor adjustments in the production process as well as in business conditions. The plant capacity in the short run is fixed and as such, it can increase its production and sales by intensive utilization of existing plants and machineries, having over time work for the existing staff etc. Thus, in the short run, a firm has its own technical and managerial constraints. But in the long run, as there is plenty of time at the disposal of a firm, it can expand and add to the existing capacities, build up new plants, employ additional workers etc to meet the rising demand in the market. Thus, in the long run, a firm will have adequate time and ample opportunity to make all kinds of adjustments and readjustments in production process and in its marketing strategies.

It is to be noted with great care that a firm has to maximize its profits after taking in to consideration of various factors in to account. They are as follows:

1. Pricing and business strategies of rival firms and its impact on the working of the given firm.
2. Aggressive sales promotion policies adopted by rival firms in the market.
3. Without inducing the workers to demand higher wages and salaries leading to rise in operation costs.
4. Without inducing the workers to demand higher wages and salaries government controls and takeovers.
5. Maintaining the quality of the product and services to the customers.
6. Taking various kings of risks and uncertainties in the changing business environment.

7. Adopting a stable business policy.
8. Avoiding any sort of clash between short run and long run profits in the business policy and maintaining proper balance between them.
9. Maintaining its reputation, name, fame and image in the market.
10. Profit maximization is necessary in both perfect and imperfect markets. In a perfect market, a firm is a price-taker and under imperfect market it becomes a price-searcher.

1.5. Game Theory

Game theory is the study of how and why individuals and entities (called players) make decisions about their situations. It is a theoretical framework for conceiving social scenarios among competing players. In some respects, game theory is the science of strategy, or at least of the optimal decision-making of independent and competing actors in a strategic setting. Game theory is used in a variety of fields to lay out various situations and predict their most likely outcomes. Businesses may use it, for example, to set prices, decide whether to acquire another firm, and determine how to handle a lawsuit.

How Game Theory Works

The goal of game theory is to explain the strategic actions of two or more players in a given situation with set rules and outcomes. Any time a situation with two or more players involves known payouts or quantifiable consequences, we can use game theory to help determine the most likely outcomes. The focus of game theory is the game, which is an interactive situation that involves rational players. The key to game theory is that one player's payoff is contingent on the strategy implemented by the other player.

The game identifies the players' identities, preferences, available strategies, and how these strategies affect the outcome. Depending on the model, various other requirements or assumptions may be necessary. Game theory has a wide range of applications, including psychology, evolutionary biology, war, politics, economics, and business. Despite its many advances, game theory is still a young and developing science.

The Nash Equilibrium

Nash equilibrium is an outcome reached that, once achieved, means no player can increase payoff by changing decisions unilaterally. It can also be thought of as a "no regrets" outcome in the sense that once a decision is made, the player will have no regrets about it, considering the consequences.

The Nash equilibrium is reached over time, normally. However, once the Nash equilibrium is reached, it will not be deviated from. In such a case, consider how a unilateral move would affect the situation. Does it make any sense? It shouldn't, and that's why the Nash equilibrium outcome is described as "no regrets."

Generally, there can be more than one equilibrium in a game. However, this usually occurs in games with more complex elements than two choices by two players. In simultaneous games that are repeated over time, one of these multiple equilibria is reached after some trial and error.

This scenario of different choices over time before reaching equilibrium is most often played out in the business world when two firms are determining prices for highly interchangeable products, such as airfare or soft drinks.

Impact of Game Theory

Game theory is present in almost every industry or field of research. Its expansive theory can pertain to many situations, making it a versatile and important theory. Here are several fields of study directly impacted by game theory.

Economics: Game theory brought about a revolution in economics by addressing crucial problems in prior mathematical economic models. For instance, neoclassical economics struggled to explain entrepreneurial anticipation and could not handle the imperfect competition. Game theory turned attention away from steady-state equilibrium toward the market process. Economists often use game theory to explain oligopoly firm behavior. It helps to predict likely outcomes when firms engage in certain behaviors, such as price-fixing and collusion.

Business: In business, game theory is beneficial for modeling competing behaviors between economic agents. Businesses often have several strategic choices that affect their ability to realize economic gain. For example, businesses may face dilemmas such as whether to retire existing products and develop new ones or employ new marketing strategies. Businesses can often choose their opponent as well. Some focus on external forces and compete against other market participants. Others set internal goals and strive to be better than their previous versions. Whether external or internal, companies are always competing for resources, attempting to hire the best candidates away from rivals, and dissuade customers from choosing competing goods. Game theory in business may most resemble a game tree, as shown below. A company may start in position one and must decide on two outcomes. However, there are continually other decisions to be made; the final payoff amount is not known until the final decision has been processed.

Project Management

Project management involves social aspects of game theory, as different participants may have different influences. For example, a project manager may be motivated to successfully complete a building development project. Meanwhile, the construction worker may be motivated to work slower for safety or to delay the project to add more billable hours. When dealing with an internal team, game theory may be less prevalent as all participants working for the same employer often have a greater shared interest for success. However, third-party consultants or external parties assisting with a project may be motivated by other factors separate from the project's success.

Consumer Product Pricing

The strategy of Black Friday shopping is at the heart of game theory. The concept holds that should companies reduce prices, more consumers will buy more goods. The relationship between a consumer, a good, and the financial exchange that transfers ownership plays a major part in game theory, as each consumer has a different set of expectations. Other than sweeping sales in advance of the holiday season, companies must utilize game theory when pricing products for launch or in anticipation of competition from rival goods. A balance must be found. Price a good too low and it won't reap profit. Price a good too high and it might push customers toward a substitute.

Types of Game Theory

Cooperative vs. Non-Cooperative Games: Although there are many types of game theory, such as symmetric/asymmetric, simultaneous/sequential, and so on, cooperative and non-cooperative game theories are the most common. Cooperative game theory deals with how coalitions, or cooperative groups, interact when only the payoffs are known. It is a game between coalitions of players rather than between individuals, and it questions how groups form and how they allocate the payoff among players. Non-cooperative game theory deals with how rational economic agents deal with each other to achieve their own goals. The most common non-cooperative game is the strategic game, in which only the available strategies and the outcomes that result from a combination of choices are listed. A simplistic example of a real-world non-cooperative game is rock-paper-scissors.

Zero-Sum vs. Non-Zero-Sum Games: When there is a direct conflict between multiple parties striving for the same outcome, it is often called a zero-sum game. This means that for every winner, there is a loser. Alternatively, it means that the collective net benefit received is equal to the collective net benefit lost. Lots of sporting events are a zero-sum game as one team wins and another team loses. A non-zero-sum game is one in which all participants can win or lose at the same time. Consider business partnerships that are mutually beneficial and foster value for both entities. Instead of competing and attempting to win at the expense of the other, both parties benefit. Investing and trading stocks is sometimes considered a zero-sum game. After all, one market participant buys a stock and another participant sells that same stock for the same price. However, because different investors have different risk appetites and investing goals, it may be mutually beneficial for both parties to transact.

Simultaneous Move vs. Sequential Move Games: Simultaneous move situations, which occur frequently in life, mean each participant must continually make decisions at the same time that their opponent is making decisions. As companies devise their marketing, product development, and operational plans, competing companies are doing the same thing at the same time. In some cases, there is an intentional staggering of decision-making steps, enabling one party to see the other party's moves before making their own. This is usually present in negotiations; one party lists their demands, then the other party has a designated amount of time to respond and list their own.

One Shot vs. Repeated Games: Game theory can begin and end in a single instance. Like much of life, the underlying competition starts, progresses, ends, and cannot be redone. This is often the case with equity traders, who must wisely choose their entry point and exit point, as their decision may not easily be undone or retried. On the other hand, some repeated games continue on and seemingly never end. These types of games often contain the same participants each time, and each party has the knowledge of what occurred previously. For example, consider rival companies trying to price their goods. Whenever one makes a price adjustment, so may the other. This circular competition repeats itself across product cycles or sale seasonality.

Types of Game Theory Strategies

Game theory participants can decide between a few primary ways to play their game. In general, each participant must decide what level of risk they are willing to take and how far they are willing to go to pursue the best possible outcome.

Maximax Strategy: A maximax strategy involves no hedging. The participant is either all in or all out; they'll either win big or face the worst consequence. Consider a new start-up company introducing new products to the market. Its new products may result in the company's market cap increasing fifty-fold. On the other hand, a failed product launch will leave the company bankrupt. The participant is willing to take a chance on achieving the best outcome even if the worst outcome is possible.

Maximin Strategy: A maximin strategy in game theory results in the participant choosing the best of the worst payoff. The participant has decided to hedge risk and sacrifice full benefit in exchange for avoiding the worst outcome. Often, companies face and accept this strategy when considering lawsuits. By settling out of court and avoiding a public trial, companies agree to an adverse outcome. However, that outcome could have been worse if the case had gone to trial.

Dominant Strategy: In a dominant strategy, a participant performs actions that are the best outcome for the play, irrespective of what other participants decide to do. In business, this may be a situation where a company decides to scale and expand to a new market, regardless of whether a competing company has decided to move into the market as well. In Prisoner's Dilemma, the dominant strategy would be to confess.

Pure Strategy: Pure strategy entails the least amount of strategic decision-making, as pure strategy is simply a defined choice that is made regardless of external forces or actions of others. Consider a game of rock-paper-scissors in which one participant decides to throw the same shape with each trial. As the outcome for this participant is well-defined in advance (outcomes are either a specific shape or not that specific shape), the strategy is defined as pure.

Mixed Strategy: A mixed strategy may seem like random chance, but there is much thought that must go into devising a plan of mixing elements or actions. Consider the relationship between a baseball pitcher and batter. The pitcher cannot throw the same pitch each time. Otherwise, the batter could predict what would come next. Instead, the pitcher must mix their strategy from pitch to pitch to create a sense of unpredictability that they hope to benefit from.

Limitations of Game Theory

The biggest issue with game theory is that, like most other economic models, it relies on the assumption that people are rational actors who are self-interested and utility-maximizing. Of course, we are social beings who do cooperate often at our own expense. Game theory cannot account for the fact that in some situations we may fall into a Nash equilibrium, and other times not, depending on the social context and who the players are. In addition, game theory often struggles to factor in human elements such as loyalty, honesty, or empathy. Though statistical and mathematical computations can dictate what a best course of action should be, humans may not take this course due to incalculable and complex scenarios of self-sacrifice or manipulation.

1.6. Oligopoly

Market structures come in different forms and sizes. The term is used to describe the distinctions between industries, which are made up of different companies that sell their products and services. Most market structures aim for perfect competition, which is a theoretical construct that doesn't actually exist. These market structures are made up of a small number of companies within an industry that controls the market. Firms in an oligopoly set prices, whether collectively—in a cartel—or under the leadership of one firm, rather than taking prices from the market. Profit margins are thus higher than they would be in a more competitive market.

Some of the barriers to entry (that prevent new players from entering the market) in an oligopoly include economies of scale, regulatory barriers, accessing supply and distribution channels, capital requirements, and brand loyalty. Oligopolies in history include steel manufacturers, oil companies, railroads, tire manufacturing, grocery store chains, and wireless carriers. The economic and legal concern is that an oligopoly can block new entrants, slow innovation, and increase prices, all of which harm consumers.

Special Considerations

Governments sometimes respond to oligopolies with laws against price-fixing and collusion. Yet, a cartel can price fix if they operate beyond the reach or with the blessing of governments. Oligopolies that exist in mixed economies often seek out and lobby for favorable government policy to operate under the regulation or even direct supervision of government agencies. The main problem that firms in an oligopoly face is that each firm has an incentive to cheat. if all firms in the oligopoly agree to jointly restrict supply and keep prices high, then each firm stands to capture substantial business from the others by breaking the agreement and undercutting the others. Such competition can be waged through prices, or through simply the individual company expanding its own output brought to market.

An oligopoly market structure is a market characterized by a small number of large firms that dominate the market. These firms have significant market power, which enables them to influence market prices and to make decisions that affect the overall market. The key characteristics of an oligopoly market structure include:

- **Few firms**: There are only a few firms in the market, which makes it easy for the firms to coordinate their behavior and to reach agreements with each other.

- **Interdependence**: The firms are interdependent and their decisions and actions affect the other firms in the market. Each firm has to consider the likely reactions of its rivals before making any decisions.
- **Barriers to entry**: There are significant barriers to entry, which prevent new firms from entering the market and competing with the existing firms. These barriers can be in the form of legal or regulatory barriers, high startup costs, or strong brand recognition.
- **Product differentiation**: The firms in an oligopoly market structure often differentiate their products from each other, either through physical differences or through advertising and marketing.
- **Non-price competition**: Firms in an oligopoly market structure often engage in non-price competition, such as advertising and product innovation, to attract customers.
- **Price rigidity**: The firms in an oligopoly market structure may engage in price collusion and maintain high prices for their products, or they may engage in price wars and lower prices to gain market share. In either case, prices tend to be rigid in the short run.

Examples of industries that exhibit oligopoly market structure include the automobile, airline, and telecommunications industries.

Demand Curve for Oligopoly

The demand curve for an oligopoly firm may have a kinked shape. The kinked demand curve model is a theory of oligopoly in which competing firms have symmetrically "kinked" demand curves. The upper part of the curve is relatively inelastic because, in response to a price increase, other firms do not follow suit, and the firm would lose a large share of its customers. The lower part of the curve is relatively elastic because, in response to a price decrease, other firms follow suit, and the firm would gain only a small share of new customers. As a result, the firm faces a discontinuity in its marginal revenue curve at the kink point, where the slope of the marginal revenue curve changes abruptly. This makes the firm less likely to change its price, and the market becomes more stable. The kinked demand curve model is used to explain price rigidity in oligopolistic markets.

Example:

Suppose there are only two firms in an industry, Firm A and Firm B, and they produce identical products. The market demand for the product is given by the following table:

Price	Quantity Demanded
10	100
20	90
30	80
40	70
50	50
60	30
70	10

Suppose further that each firm has a marginal cost curve that is upward sloping and intersects the average total cost curve at a point below the kink in the demand curve. This means that each firm has an incentive to produce at the level where its marginal cost equals its marginal revenue, up to the point where the kink occurs in the demand curve.

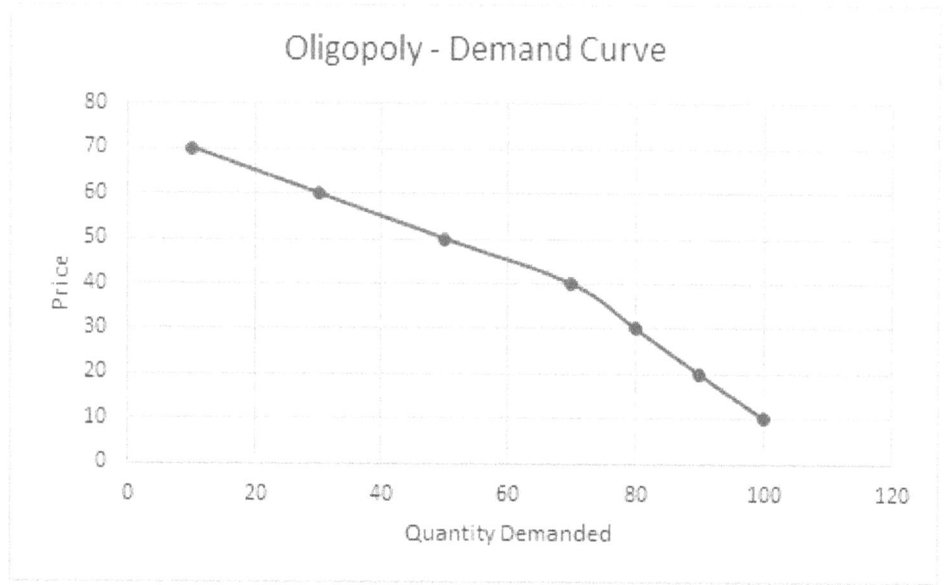

The kink in the demand curve occurs at a price of 40, where the demand curve becomes more elastic above the price and less elastic below the price. This kink reflects the assumption that if one firm were to raise its price above 40, it would lose a large share of its sales to the other firm, which would keep its price at 40 or lower. On the other hand, if one firm were to lower its price below 40, the other firm would follow suit, and both firms would end up with lower profits. Therefore, both firms have an incentive to keep their prices around 40.

This kinked demand curve implies that the oligopoly market may be relatively stable, with prices and quantities staying roughly constant over time. However, it also implies that the market may be prone to sudden changes in prices and quantities if one firm decides to deviate from the tacitly agreed upon price.

Unique features of Oligopoly

Oligopoly is a market structure characterized by a small number of large firms dominating the market, each having significant market power. Here are some unique features of oligopoly firms:

Price leadership: In an oligopoly, one firm may emerge as the dominant player, known as the price leader. The other firms in the market tend to follow the price leader's pricing strategy, which may lead to price stability in the market.

Cartel: Oligopoly firms may also form a cartel, which is a group of firms that work together to coordinate their pricing and output decisions. Cartels can be illegal, as they reduce competition and raise prices for consumers.

Game theory: Game theory is a tool used to study the behavior of firms in an oligopoly. In an oligopoly, firms must take into account how their competitors will respond to their pricing and output decisions, as their actions will impact the profits of other firms in the market.

Duopoly: Duopoly is a special case of oligopoly where there are only two firms in the market. In a duopoly, the actions of one firm directly impact the profits of the other firm, and this interdependence can lead to strategic behavior such as price wars and collusion.

Overall, the unique features of oligopoly firms arise from the fact that there are only a few large firms dominating the market, and these firms must take into account the behavior of their competitors when making pricing and output decisions.

Advantages and Disadvantages of an Oligopoly

Advantages: One of the main benefits of having an oligopoly is that competition is very limited. That's because there are very few players in the market. Since there are few competitors, an oligopoly allows those who participate to net a higher amount of profits.

Disadvantages: Oligopolies come with higher barriers to entry for new participants. This means that it can be difficult to enter the market because of the high costs associated with doing business, the regulatory environment, and the problems that arise when it comes to accessing supply and distribution channels. Because of the lack of competition, there may be very little incentive to innovate product and service offerings. With no diversity in offerings, consumers remain loyal to what they know best.

Chapter 2: Strategy Formulation

Business strategy involves making and executing critical choices regarding where to play and how to win. Strategy Formulation will help you understand and make these important strategic choices for your company to compete and win in the marketplace.

2.1. Creating Great Strategy

Managing a multibusiness organization means managing the relationship between executives in the central office and those who run the business units or divisions. And strategy gurus notwithstanding, there is no one best way to do that. Rather, the best way always depends on the nature and needs of the businesses in a company's portfolio, on the styles of the people in the corporate office, on the company's strategy and goals. Strength of this style is that it encourages strategies that are well integrated across business units. The close involvement of central managers, strong staff functions, and overlapping responsibilities make it possible for the units to coordinate their plans. Doing so is especially important when business areas are linked through shared resources, for instance, or common distribution networks.

Perhaps the greatest strength of the strategic planning style is that it fosters the creation of ambitious business strategies. Strategic planning companies are most effective in helping business units strive to gain advantage over competitors. Once headquarters establishes the direction in which the business should be going, unit managers are free to develop bold plans to achieve whatever goal has been set. "We would never have been able to pursue such an ambitious strategy if we were an independent company," one business unit manager in a strategic planning company told us. And that statement characterizes the thinking of many similarly situated unit managers. Moreover, because the strategic objectives come from the top, the units can support those objectives without great concern for the short-term financial impact of their actions. They are, in a sense, buffered from capital market pressures. Finally, at its best, the agreement between the corporate office and the business unit creates a shared purpose that helps motivate those who must carry out the plan.

Great strategies accomplish this with the following characteristics:

- **Simple:** Reshapes complexity to be manageable and actionable.
- **Candid:** Dares to spotlight the most difficult truths.
- **Decisive:** Asserts clear decisions and accepts their consequences.
- **Leveraged:** Magnifies strengths into durable competitive advantage.
- **Asymmetric:** Defeats uncertainty with higher upside than downside.
- **Futuristic:** Solves for the long-term.

The world is complex, and therefore difficult to reason about. Strategy intentionally omits detail in exchange for clarity. Armed with a simple narrative, mere mortals can achieve understanding, and make every-day decisions that remain aligned to that narrative. No one reads anything. You're in the Top 1% just for reading this sentence. No one remembers anything. Certainly not an 86-slide PowerPoint[1]. So the strategy has to be simple—even simplistic—to have a chance at being read or remembered.

People are mired in their day to day work; only when the strategy is simple, does it have a chance of being incorporated. Only when the context is over-simplified, having made scrutable the complexity of the real world, can we easily explain "why," and retell those stories in our weekly meetings and prioritization sessions. Those are the places where strategy lives and breathes, where teams can move quickly, independently, fulfilling their individual missions with a minimum of coordination, yet all supporting a common theory for how we will win, together. If the strategy is simple, it might appear obvious. If it is obvious, it might appear uninsightful. Humans assume that complex puzzles require complex answers, when in fact often the simplest answer is the best answer. "Obviousness" is a sign of a strategy that not only is easy to communicate and execute, but also believed.

Its job isn't to be non-obvious, but rather to cleanly specify what is most important. It might be obvious to do X, but Y and Z are also "obvious," so by selecting X and not Y nor Z, you have created focus, and specified "how to win." Simplicity at its worst becomes reductive—overlooking complexity rather than tackling it, resulting in conclusions that, while admittedly simple and clear, are wrong. We cannot pretend that complex problems can always be waved away by simple statements. The process of strategy creation must indeed tackle the complexity of the world, but the output of that process is a document that frees everyone else from having to re-solve every puzzle. Like a street map, we omit detail in exchange for clarity of the most important context and routes. Simplicity that ignores reality is reductive, but simplicity that arises from an exceptional summarization of having already processed the messy, complex world, is elegant. Characterizing the world in a few, simple, clear assertions, and solving our challenges with a few, clear directives of what we must do, is required for a strategy to be "how we will win."

Candid

Strategy must lay bare the most frightening, embarrassing realities. It must face the truth that we all avoid facing during the struggle of daily work. If the strategy doesn't expose—and then solve—the most brutal facts, the strategy is wrong. In particular, the strategy must diagnose the primary challenges facing the business, even if the facts are so scary that it seems hopeless. Existential threats are the most important to articulate. Too often a strategy claims "threats" that are lazy, generic, non-actionable pseudo-concerns that nearly every company could claim, like "Google could copy us" or "A new startup could invent a great product and get huge funding" or "A massive security breach could cause half our customers to leave." Real threats are either happening now or are at least 70% likely to happen. Real threats are specific, ideally backed by data that proves they are happening, e.g. your market is shrinking; a competitor has accelerating market share; cancellation rates prove that even paying customers don't value the product. Real threats are written in the present tense because they are happening, not hypothetically with "could" or "might."

When the puzzles are clear, everyone can help solve them. When the puzzles remain hidden, what's the chance that they'll be solved by accident? If you're worried someone might leave the company when they hear how scary it is, maybe they should leave the company. These are the challenges we're facing together; if they're not willing to solve them, they need to make space for someone who will relish the challenge. Not just for the company's sake but for their own happiness and fulfillment. Facing the truth, being specific about current reality and about what needs to be done, is required for a strategy to be "how we will win."

Decisive

A strategy asserts a set of justified, self-consistent decisions, such as:

- Which subsets of the market to target and conversely which we'll ignore, even if some of those sign up as customers anyway, and ask for things we're not going to do, and then cancel in anger

- Which customer personas are most important to delight and conversely which will dislike our product, causing us no dismay, whose feature-requests we will quickly close as "won't do" rather than wring our hands at all the features we still need to build
- How to position against the competition and conversely where the competition will be stronger, unlike those fake-news marketing charts comparing our product with the competition, where only our product scores 100% along every dimension
- What we value (e.g. quality, service, speed, design, compatibility, lock-in) and conversely what we will give up, e.g. releasing features faster but of lower quality, or being infinitely extensible versus top-to-bottom thoughtful design
- What we must (and must not) build, to pay off that positioning and win those customers in that market.

There are both positive and negative second-order consequences of any complex decision. If these aren't identified—in particular, if the problematic consequences aren't embraced within the strategy—then it's not a clear decision. When those consequences inevitably arise, the team must be able to say we expected that rather than we have to address that or even this is a signal that the strategy is wrong. A common tactic for avoiding making a decision is to use non-specific language. "We will leverage synergies to create unique solutions" is, in fact, a good thing to do, but it doesn't specify which synergies to leverage, what is unique about it, or what the unique solution is. Fluffy language is a hallmark of indecisiveness, and therefore of bad strategy. Being specific is good marketing, anyway.

The opposite of the decision must also be a rational choice, made by other successful organizations. For example, deciding to be open source is strategic, because plenty of companies are successful with a closed-source strategy. However, deciding to be "customer-first" is not a serious decision, because successful companies don't use a "customer-last" strategy. This "Opposite Test" is useful both to form proper strategic decisions, and to form great positioning statements for marketing. Decisions and consequences must at minimum be self-consistent. If you've decided to have a low price, you can't also have white-glove service. If you've decided that everything requires high-quality design, you can't also release features faster than the competition. Or, perhaps you can creatively build a solution that does say "yes to both" of those things, but only by also accepting additional constraints that resolve the conflict.

Better than "self-consistent" is "mutually-reinforcing." This means that one decision makes another more powerful, or easier, or less expensive, and vice versa, so that adhering to both makes you far stronger than having only one. For example, deciding to have only a few features, and also amazing design. Normally customers might not put up with less functionality, but if the design experience is exceptional, they might be happy with something that "does only a few things, but so delightfully!" And vice versa: It's easier to execute on great design when you don't have to tackle a complex product with tons of use-cases and personas and functionality.

Leveraged

"Leverage" means generating a large effect from a relatively small effort, where time and dollars are far more effective than one might expect, because we are riding tailwinds of natural abilities or hard-won assets, rather than fighting a battle against so-called "weaknesses." You know you're leveraging strengths when you see other people shake their heads in amazement at how much you accomplished in so little time.

It's good to leverage strengths. Much literature on strategy dwells on how to create moats—permanent competitive advantages—but so many organizations still aren't leveraging the straightforward, undifferentiated strengths that they possess. They expend most of their energy shoring up "weaknesses," which despite their efforts will at best become "less weak," but never become a strength. Whereas applying that same energy in leveraging their strengths will have a large positive effect. It's even just more fun to play to your strengths instead of wallowing in weaknesses. It is of course better when the strength is differentiated from the competition. This is especially obvious in a mature market where everyone is saying the same things on their home page, pricing the same way, and different only in tertiary characteristics. Winning in your own way can defeat "better" competitors. It's even better when that differentiation is durable over time. It has never been more difficult to establish a permanent advantage, when all software can be reproduced, all business models can be replicated, and the entire world is both your market and your competitors, which makes it all the more important to decide what one or two moats you will build. The strategy is the place to name those moats.

Tailoring the decisions for the strengths of this organization, avoiding (rather than reversing) weaknesses, even better when the strength is differentiated, identifying and investing in durable differentiation, so that moats are constructed in the long run, is required for a strategy to be "how we will win.

Asymmetric

This remarkable fact is due to its asymmetrical shape: it is pointy at the front and flat in the back. This creates resistance to moving backwards, but a natural ease in moving forward. Even when the water is randomly undulating, "backward" forces are muted, while "forward" forces are allowed, so the boat glides forward. Asymmetries can amplify positive effects while muting negative ones, resulting in a net-positive force even under conditions of random inputs. Great strategies prescribe activities that always move the company forward, despite the inevitable bad luck and setbacks. To do that, the activities must exhibit asymmetry, where the upside vastly exceeds the cost, so that even if you took 2x longer to achieve 50% of what you expected, you still win.

This is the mechanism behind Venture Capital portfolios, which are investments in a slate of early-stage startups. The worst-case outcome for each bet is that they lose 100% of their investment, but in the best case they can gain 10,000%. A few large successes more than make up for the many failures, so the portfolio in total comes out positive. Investors call these asymmetric bets. Economists call this convexity. Strategy must create a portfolio of bets having this VC-like asymmetric quality, whether for a small startup trying to find product/market fit or a mature company entering new markets. A sign of a bad strategy is when success requires everything to go right. With a set of asymmetric bets, the successes render the failures moot, and so the unpredictable waves crashing into the boat still result in forward motion.

One form of asymmetric bet is entering a large and growing market. Besides the obvious benefits there is the asymmetry of optionality: There are many niches to exploit, many possible ways for a product to deliver value, many marketing and sales channels, and there's more of all of it every year. Because there are many options to try, there are many ways to succeed; if your first few ideas don't work, the next one might. By having lots of ways to succeed, you are more likely to find one. Waves on the boat.

Another kind of asymmetry is a process that compounds, meaning that the more of it there is, the faster it grows. Things with this characteristic naturally grow larger than anything that grows in a more linear fashion, even if they start out small. Examples are customer retention, customer upgrades, and employee retention. Another example is a growth-vector that is proportional to the size of the current customer base, such as word of mouth referrals and viral products (e.g. once you join a social platform or collaborative online tool, you tend to get other people you know to join as well). Most things that grow non-linearly don't grow exponentially—that's normal, and still a great strategy.

Every plan will face challenges, both foreseeable and bad luck. If everything has to go right for the plan to succeed, it won't succeed. Whether a single investment has asymmetric upside, or a portfolio of bets collectively has large upside, exploiting asymmetries maximizes the chance that the strategy will succeed despite the inevitable travails and uncontrollable luck, and thus is vital to "how we will win.

Futuristic

Don't pretend you can predict the future, assume the quantity of "things we don't know" is larger than the quantity "things we do know," iterate quickly on hypotheses that you proactively attempt to disprove, and adjust in the presence of new information. The team that learns the fastest, wins. The team that spends three months trying predict the future, is now three months behind, and the future still won't unfold as they predicted. Being agile is a great way to climb the proverbial mountain-shrouded-in-fog. Some paths are the right ones, but backtracking is inevitable; it's a sign of puzzling-out, not a sign of failure. The job of strategy is to identify which mountain we're trying to climb in the first place—the puzzle we're solving for, the opportunity we're exploiting. If an "agile, self-managed" team climbs the wrong mountain, it was all a waste.

Strategy looks further into the future than anything else at the company. Therefore, it has the responsibility to take the long view. Which is especially difficult, as the future is unpredictable, and data tells you about the past, but rarely about the future. If you can solve a problem in a month, you probably should, but that also means it's not a strategic problem. Anything that can be built in three months, isn't the way you will have constructed a moat that will take competitors years to overcome. Anything that specifies features or timelines is a roadmap, not a strategy; a strategy specifies market and business outcomes and the primary decisions and secondary consequences. Anything that specifies teams or roles or hiring or processes is an operational plan, not a strategy; a strategy details the outcomes and activities that require the entire company to accomplish together, not what one team needs to accomplish alone.

The Vision statement is often the first sentence the strategy document, but was the last thing crafted by the authors of that document. Only once you fully understand the challenges you face, the main, coherent courses of actions to undertake, and the results you want, can you summarize a clear vision of what the future will be. Strategy is where we specify the most critical long-term challenges facing the company, and the rocks that are the most important things, not to win the battles today, but to determine how we will have won the war three years from now, how we will achieve our vision, how we will win.

Bad Strategy

Tell-tale signs of a strategy that lacks these qualities:

Not simple: Pages of detail. Slides with more than 20 words. A litany of numbers without a narrative explaining what insights they create. No diagrams "painting the picture," or diagrams with 20 boxes. Too many points for someone to recall from memory. Important concepts that aren't summarized by a short phrase that people can use as a daily short-hand.

Not candid: Nothing where the future of the company hangs in the balance. Nothing that makes the reader say, "Oh wow, dang, what are we going to do about that!?" Nothing scary that demands action. No serious consequence if the directives aren't followed. A reader who finishes the document and thinks, "We're still ignoring the elephant in the room."

Not decisive: No clear decisions that would cause us to "easily say 'no'" to many otherwise excellent, reasonable ideas. Not obvious what we're not doing. Non-specific target market (e.g. "for everyone"), target customer (e.g. "any [title]"), target jobs-to-be-done. Directives and headings using the word "and" to expand scope rather than limiting it. No negative-but-accepted consequences of the decisions. Decisions that conflict with each other. Decisions that don't reinforce each other.

Not leveraged: Strategy would apply equally well to a competitor, or even to a business in another industry. Strategy doesn't call out the special strengths and durable assets of the organization, or doesn't explain how to apply them to win, especially how it will position against the competition. No obvious moats being constructed. No network of interlocking decisions that together makes the company special. Demanding that the organization overcome more than one or two major deficiencies.

Not asymmetric: Potential upsides aren't at least 10x larger than costs. Linear cost/reward, or risk/reward. Not creating optionality in how each aspect can go right, leading to one thing that absolutely must work. A course of action that requires multiple different, difficult things to simultaneously go right, otherwise the whole strategy fails.

Not futuristic: Doesn't describe a specific future destination of the company or product. A "vision" that describes what the company already does and already is, rather than how things will be different once we successfully execute our strategy. Doesn't specify which moats are being created, and how. Specifies teams, products, timelines, or features. Deals with temporary challenges that can be solved in a quarter rather than long-term challenges that will take years to fully overcome. Describes how to win this year instead of in three years. Relies primarily on data to predict the future.

Not strategy (bonus): Generic statements that would apply equally to nearly any company, even in a different field (e.g. grow faster, lower attrition, hire the best talent, delight customers, beat the competition). Aspirations about what we wish would happen, without specifying how it will happen. Financial goals rather than how to win competitive markets. Plans that are in someone's head instead of written down and shared. Written documents that aren't referenced when creating plans.

2.2. Industry Analysis as Input to Strategy

The purpose of strategic management is to create competitive advantage. But how do companies know they have competitive advantage? In the long term, competitive advantage will lead to greater profitability. But in the shorter term, it is difficult for companies to assess how well they are creating competitive advantage. An industry analysis is a method for a company to assess its market position relative to its competitors. An industry analysis is meant to help a company review various market and financial factors in its industry that affect the business, including evaluating the competition. This analysis helps managers understand the important factors of the marketplace and how these factors may be used to gain a competitive advantage. Industry analyses are an important tool for companies to assess their strategy in a shorter time frame. Because conditions in the business environment are constantly changing, industry analyses need to be done periodically to keep up with developments. This can be a very time-consuming process and, if not done accurately, can lead to bad strategic decisions. For this reason, managers may go to outside firms, either to produce the analysis or to provide data for the company to complete an analysis. A number of companies exist that maintain huge databases of information about particular industries, such as Hoovers and IBIS. These companies have methods for gathering the data and for analyzing the data to produce reports.

Components of Industry Analysis and Factors

Impact of the Company's Industry Environment on Its Competitive Advantage

The industry environment comprises mainly of three components:

Component

Customers: Effective strategists are concerned with their customers, their needs and desires, their potential customers and their location as well as the trends in the future that may lead to changes in customer buying patterns. In fact, opportunities come through identifying and providing for customer needs and desires, and threats come from failures to meet changing customer needs.

The various issues concerning to customers and potential customers relate to three factors as follows:

(a) Customer identification,

(b) Demographic factors and

(c) Geographic location of markets.

(a) Customer Identification:

Customers show their interest in a product or service for a variety of reasons. They purchase a product or service because it satisfies their needs, desires or requirements. Marketers generally describe three distinct classes of customers - consumers, retailers and/or wholesalers and industrial and/or institutional buyers.

Each of these groups has somewhat different factors that affect their purchase decisions. Factors as availability of a product or service, its price, variety, convenience, quality, warranty, easiness of credit and reputation generally influence consumers.

Retailers and/or wholesalers decide in favor of a product or service because of competitiveness of a product or service, product availability, product turnover, product line breadth, consumer recognition, profit potential, promotional and merchandising support and supply dependability.

Cost vs. profitability, price, product performance, product line, product information, source availability, legal conformity, and financing, technical assistance influence the industrial and/or institutional buyers.

These factors vary in importance. For example, industrial buyers of durable goods may be more concerned with setup or maintenance costs of equipment as a factor in their own profitability and less concerned with price. These same purchasers may be very price-sensitive to commodities as pens or paper. Therefore, consumer products firms adapt their strategies as consumer needs shift and as demographic changes take place.

Corporate strategists identify the nature of the customers, their needs and desire in order to avoid threats of loss of customers and create opportunities for them to find new customers or sell more to existing ones. Again, these customers and their needs are constantly changing.

(b) Demographic Factors:

Several important conditions associated with the general population affect the market for goods and services for different industries. Marketers refer to these as "primary demand factors". Changes in population, age shifts in the population and income distribution of the population are the most important of the factors that create threats and opportunities, and affect strategies of different types of firms in different industries.

(c) Geographic Factors:

An effective strategist also examines the geographic environment to identify opportunities and threats as part of analyzing the customer sector. The strategist has essentially to determine if conditions are better elsewhere for achieving corporate objectives. He seeks new locations to add to current location or search for areas to relocate.

Sometimes a change involves moving corporate headquarters to a new region. It could also mean moving the plant or operations location from the city to a suburb or from one city to another.

Thus in the customer sector of the industry environment, the firm's strategy must be related with its customers and their needs and desires, changes in their purchase patterns and their location.

Component

Suppliers:

Suppliers of a firm provide capital, labor, materials, and so on to a firm. Effective strategists are concerned with supplier changes in the environment, cost and availability of all the factors of production, raw materials, subassemblies, money, energy and employees. The power relationships between the firm and the suppliers affect them. The power of buyer also affects the cost of supplies.

Component

Competitors:

The strategists must also assess the state of competition in the industry environment. For this determines whether a firm will remain in its current business and what strategies it will follow in pursuing its business.

Three factors must be examined regarding competition:

(1) Entry and exit of major competitors

(2) Substitutes and complements for current products and services

(3) Major strategic changes by current competitors

Competitive Forces Model

Managers face the task of analyzing competitive forces in an industry environment in order to identify the opportunities and threats confronting a company. Michael Porter argues that a corporation is most concerned with the intensity of competition within its industry. Basic competitive forces in the industry determine the level of this intensity.

"The collective strength of these forces determines the ultimate profit potential in the industry, where profit potential is measured in terms of long-run return on invested capital." At the time of scanning its industry environment, a company must assess the importance to its success of each of the basic forces.

Porter has mentioned five of these forces, to which Wheelen and Hunger have added six one: The model is designed to help the analysis of the basic posture of competition in any industry, by taking a broader look at the forces of competition and bringing together a number of different factors in a convenient model.

The model focuses on six forces that shape competition within an industry:

1. The threat of potential entry from outside the industry

2. The degree of rivalry among companies within an industry.

3. The bargaining power of buyers,

4. The bargaining power of suppliers, and

5. The threat posed by industries producing substitute goods or services.

6. Other stakeholders

The sixth force reflects the power that governments, local communities, and other groups from the task environment wield over industry activities. The stronger each of these forces, the more limited companies are in their ability to raise prices and earn greater profits.

The development of a viable strategy, therefore, should first involve the identification and evaluation of all six forces. The nature and importance of these forces vary from industry to industry and from company to company. The strategy, should, then aim to protect the firm from the resultant dangers.

The strength of these forces limits the ability of established companies to raise prices and earn higher profits. A strong competitive force can be regarded as a threat since it reduces profit. A weak competitive force can be considered as an opportunity, for it permits a company to earn greater profits. In the short run, these forces act as constraints on a company's activities.

In the long run, however, it may be possible for a company, through its choice of strategy, to change the strength of one or more of the forces to the company's advantage. The task of a strategic manager is to recognize opportunities and threats as they arise and to formulate appropriate strategic responses.

A strategist can evaluate any industry by rating each competitive force as high, medium or low in strength. For example, the rivalry in the athletic shoe industry could be rated as high where Nike, Reebok, Adidas, and Converse are strong competitors worldwide; threat of potential entrants is low where industry has reached maturity and sales growth rate has slowed; threat of substitutes is low because other does do not provide support for sports activities; bargaining power of suppliers is medium but rising as suppliers in Asian countries are increasing in size and ability; bargaining power of buyers is medium but increasing as the popularity of athletic shoes is dropping; threat of other stakeholders is medium to high because of growing government regulations and concern for human rights.

On the basis of current trends in each of these competitive forces, it can be inferred that the industry appears to be increasing in its level of competitive intensity leading to falling profit margins for the industry as a whole.

When this risk is low, companies can charge higher prices and earn greater profits. Companies more likely pursue strategies consistent with these aims. The height of barriers to entry is the most important determinant of profit rates in an industry.

Pharmaceuticals, house- hold detergents, and commercial jet aircraft are the examples of industries where entry barrier are considerable/high. Pharmaceuticals and household detergents industries have achieved product differentiation through substantial expenditures for research and development and advertising and have built brand loyalty, making it difficult for new companies to enter these industries on a significant scale.

The differential strategies of Procter and Gamble and Unilever have been so successful in house- hold detergents that these two companies dominate the global industry. In case of commercial jet aircraft industry, the barriers to entry are primarily due to scale economies. In some industries, scale economies are extremely important, for example, in the car or airline industry.

Competitive Force 1. Entry of Potential Competitors:

Potential competitors are companies that currently are not competing in an industry but have the capability to do so if they choose. These new entrants to an industry typically bring to it new capacity, a desire to gain market share, and substantial resources. They are, therefore, threats to an established company.

Established companies in an industry try to discourage potential competitors from entering, since the more companies enter an industry, the more difficult it becomes for established companies to keep their share of the market and generate profits.

New entrants to an industry typically bring to it new capacity, a desire to gain market share, and substantial resources. They are, therefore, threats to established companies. On the other hand, if the risk of new entry is low, established companies could take advantage of this opportunity to raise prices and earn greater returns.

The threat of entry depends on the presence of entry barriers and the reaction that can be expected from existing competitors. An entry barrier is an obstruction that makes it difficult for a company to enter an industry.

The barriers to entry imply that there are significant costs to joining an industry. The higher the costs the potential entrants must bear, the greater are the barriers to entry. High entry barriers keep potential competitors out of an industry even when industry returns are high.

Three main sources of entry barriers:

i. Economies of scale

ii. Brand Loyalty

iii. Absolute Cost Advantages

Some more entry barriers are added:

iv. Switching Costs

v. Capital Requirements

vi. Access to Distribution Channels, and

vii. Product Differentiation

viii. Government Policy

i. Economies of Scale:

The scale economies result in saving. They are the cost advantages associated with large company size and determine the returns to scale. The cost reductions gained through mass-production of a standard output, discounts on purchases of raw material inputs and component parts in large quantities, the spreading of fixed costs over a large volume and scale economies in advertising are the sources of scale economies.

If these cost advantages are significant, then new entrants face the problem of either entering on a small scale or bear a significant cost disadvantage or take a very large risk by entering on a large scale and bearing significant capital costs.

The large- scale entry of new entrants, increasing the supply of products, will bring down prices and result in vigorous retaliation by established companies. If established companies have economies of scale, the threat of new entrants is reduced.

ii. Brand Loyalty:

The companies that have created brand loyalty for their products, have an absolute cost advantage with respect to potential competitors. Brand loyalty is defined as 'buyers' preference for the products of incumbent companies'. Continuous advertising of brand and company names, patent protection of production, product innovation through company research and development programs, an emphasis on high product quality, and good after-sales service can create brand loyalty for a company.

New entrants cannot take market share away from established companies if they have created brand loyalty. Thus brand loyalty reduces the threat of entry by new competitors since they may find the task of breaking down well- established consumer preference as too costly.

iii. Absolute Cost Advantages:

When established companies enjoy lower absolute costs it becomes difficult for potential competitors to match. Superior production techniques can give rise to absolute cost advantages. Past experience, patents, or secret processes, control of particular inputs required for production, such as labor, materials, equipment, or management skills or access to cheaper funds can be the techniques to achieve cost advantages. If established companies have an absolute cost advantages, the threat of entry decreases.

To a large extent cost advantages have to do with entries in to market and the experience so gained. It is difficult for a competitor to break into a market if there is an established operator who knows that market well, has good relationships with the key buyers and suppliers and knows how to overcome market and operating problems.

iv. Switching Costs:

Once software program like Excel or Word becomes established in an office, office managers are very reluctant to switch to a new program because of the high training costs.

v. Capital Requirements:

The need to invest huge financial resources in manufacturing facilities in order to produce large commercial airplanes creates a significant barrier to entry to any competitor for Boeing and Airbus.

vi. Access to Distribution Channels:

Small entrepreneurs often find it difficult to get supermarket shelf space for their goods because large retailers charge for space on their shelves and give priority to the established firms who pay for advertising required to generate high customer demand.

vii. Differentiation:

Differentiation means the provision of a product or service regarded by the user as meaningfully different from the competitors. The organizations that are able to achieve differentiation provide for themselves real barriers to competitive entry.

viii. Government Policy:

Governments can restrict entry into an industry through licensing requirements by restricting access to raw materials, such as oil-drilling sites in protected areas.

Competitive Force 2. Rivalry among Existing Firms in an Industry:

Companies will also be related with the extent of rivalry among competing firms in an industry. In most industries, companies are mutually dependent and a competitive move by one firm can be expected to have a noticeable effect on its competitors and thus may cause counter moves.

The rivalry among the competing sellers in an industry will be most intense where entry is likely, substitutes threaten, or buyers or suppliers exercise control.

Companies have to face each other's competitive initiatives using the tools of product introduction and innovation, pricing, quality, features, services, marketing campaigns, the use of distribution, and the like.

The intensity of rivalry among competing sellers is related to a number of factors:

i. There exist a large number of competitors that are comparable in size and power, making it more difficult for a competitor to gain dominance over another and for stability to be reached.

ii. There is a lack of product differentiation or high switching costs, forcing all companies to fight for exactly the same market. There is little to stop customers switching between sellers.

iii. When there are high fixed costs, creating a strong temptation to cut prices to increase capacity utilization.

iv. If there exist capacity indivisibilities, high exit barriers and excess capacity it will result in increased competition

v. The pace with which competitors can respond to any given initiative, as the faster they can do so, the smaller the reward is from any such initiative.

vi. Competitors dissatisfied with their current position and eager to improve it by launching destabilizing offensive attacks.

vii. Competitors diverse in terms of resources, styles, strategies, priorities and personalities, with different ideas of how to compete.

viii. An industry experiencing slow growth may increase rivalry if it is entering maturity and competitors are eager to establish themselves as market leaders.

The extent of rivalry also determines the organizational performance. The weak competitive force among companies within an industry encourages companies to charge higher price and earn greater profits.

But the strong competitive force implying significant price competition may enrage price war among companies within an industry. Price competition by lowering down the profit margins reduces the profitability of the companies.

The intensity of rivalry within an industry is mainly a function of three factors:

(a) Demand conditions,

(b) The height of exit barriers in the industry, and

(c) Industry competitive structure

(a) Demand Conditions:

The demand conditions within an industry also determine the intensity of rivalry among companies operating within an industry. Growing demand tends to moderate competition by providing greater space for expansion and reduces rivalry because all companies can sell more without taking market share away from other companies and result in high profits. Demand grows when the market as a whole is growing.

This may be when the new consumer starts consuming or the existing consumers increase usage of an industry's product. If demand is growing, companies can have increased revenues without taking market share away from the competitors. Thus growing demand provides a company a major opportunity to expand operations.

On the other hand, falling demand increases competition among the companies to maintain their market share and revenues. Demand reduces when consumers are leaving the market or when the existing consumers are buying less.

When demand is declining, a company can achieve growth only by snatching market share away from other companies. Thus declining demand presents a major threat, for it increases the extent of rivalry between established companies.

(b) Exit Barriers:

Exit barriers pose a major competitive threat when industry demand is falling. 'Exit barriers are economic, strategic, and emotional factors that keep companies competing in an industry even when returns are low.'

If exit barriers are high, companies find it difficult to leave an unprofitable industry. Excess productive capacity can occur and lead to intensified price competition. Companies can engage in cutting prices in order to obtain the orders necessary to utilize their idle capacity.

The following are the common exit barriers:

1. Investments in plant and equipment that have no alternative uses.

2. High fixed costs of exit, such as severance of pay redundant employees.

3. Company management's emotional attachment to an industry.

4. When a company is not diversified and relies economically on the industry.

5. There is strategic relationship between business units.

For example the steel industry has experienced the negative competitive effects of high exit barriers. Declining demand conditions combined with new low-cost sources of supply resulted in overcapacity in the steel industry during the late 1980s. Thus high exit barriers prevented the companies to leave the industry, which threatened the profitability of all companies within the steel industry.

(c) Industry Competitive Structure:

The competitive structure of an industry means the number and size distribution of companies operating in an industry. Different competitive structures have different implications for rivalry among companies within an industry. Industry structures range from fragmented to consolidated. "A fragmented industry contains a large number of small or medium-sized companies, none of which is in a position to dominate the industry."

Agriculture, video rental, and health clubs, real state brokers are examples of fragmented industry. "A consolidated industry is dominated by a small number of large companies" Aerospace, automobiles and pharmaceuticals are examples of consolidated industry.

Fragmented industries enjoy low entry barriers and are characterized by commodity- type products that are difficult to differentiate. This results in boom- and -bust cycles. Whenever the demand is strong, profits rise. The entry barriers being low, new firms enter into the industry hoping to cash in on the boom. The flood of new entrants creates excess capacity leading to price cuts in order to utilize excess- capacity.

The price war wipes out industry profits and compels some companies to leave the industry, and prevents potential entrants. A fragmented industry structure, thus, constitutes a threat rather than an opportunity.

Most booms will be relatively short-lived because of the ease of new entry followed by price wars and bankruptcies. Since product differentiation is often difficult in these industries, the best strategy to pursue may be cost minimization that allows a company to take advantage of high profits in a boom and survive in recession.

The nature and intensity of competition in consolidated industries are not easy to predict. The companies in the consolidated industries are interdependent. The competitive actions of one company directly affect the market share and profitability of other companies in the industry.

For instance, in 1986, the cut-rate financing by General Motors immediately affected adversely the sales and profits of Chrysler Corp. and Ford Motor Co. In order to protect their own market share, these companies had to introduce similar packages.

Obviously, in consolidated industries the interdependence of companies and the possibility of a price war constitute a major threat. In order to encounter this threat, companies often follow the price determined by a dominant company in the industry.

More often, when price wars are a threat, companies resort to non-price competition such as quality of the product and design features. This is a step towards building brand loyalty and reduces the possibility of a price war.

However, the effect of this strategy depends upon the differentiation of the industry's product. Although some products (such as automobiles) are relatively easy to differentiate, others (such as airline travel) are very difficult to differentiate.

Competitive Force 3. The Bargaining Power of Buyers:

Buyers affect an industry through their ability to force down prices, bargain for higher quality or more services, and play competitors against each other. To do this, they may refuse to buy from any single producer.

Alternatively, weak buyers give a company the opportunity to raise prices and earn greater returns. Whether buyers are able to make demands on a company depends on their power relative to that of the company.

A buyer or a group of buyers is powerful if some of the following factors hold true:

i. The buyers are concentrated (i.e. they are few in number and large in size). This allows the buyers to dominate suppliers.

ii. When the buyers purchase in bulk, they can bargain for price reductions.

iii. When the buyers buy a large percentage of the total order of the supply industry.

iv. When the buyers can switch orders between supply companies at a low cost.

v. Alternative suppliers are plentiful because the product is standard or undifferentiated for example, motorists can choose among many gas stations.

vi. When the buyers use the threat to supply their own needs through backward integration as a device for forcing down prices.

vii. If the quality of the product is not particularly important

viii.If there are readily available substitutes

ix. A buyer has the potential to integrate backward by producing the product itself.

Buyers exercise their bargaining power if they earn low profits, as they will earn low profits. This will create an incentive to lower purchasing costs or otherwise squeeze the industry, or to attempt to share its profit; for example, by backward integration.

The firm can limit the power of buyers by targeting and selling to buyers who possess the least power to influence it adversely. In general, companies can only sell profitably in the long run to powerful buyers when it produces at a low cost and its product is adequately differentiated. If the company lacks both these characteristics, each sale to a power buyer makes the company more vulnerable. In such circumstances, targeting and selling to the weaker buyers becomes very important

Competitive Force 4. The Bargaining Power of Suppliers:

Suppliers can exercise their bargaining power and affect an industry through their ability to raise prices or by reducing the quality of the product or service supplied, including delivery schedules etc. Alternatively, weak suppliers provide a company the opportunity to force down prices and demand higher quality. As with buyers, the ability of suppliers to make demands on a company depends on their power relative to that of the company.

Supplier power is likely to be high if:

i. There is concentration of suppliers than a fragmented source of supply.

ii. If its product is not a standard commodity but is unique, or at least differentiated;

iii. If the supplier's product makes up a sizeable fraction of the cost of an industry's product;

iv. When the product that suppliers sell has few substitutes and is crucial to the industry's production process

v. When the company's industry is not an important customer to the suppliers. In such instances, the supplier's health does not depend on the company's industry, and suppliers have little incentive to reduce prices or improve quality.

vi. When supplier's respective products are differentiated to such an extent that it is costly for a company to switch from one supplier to another. In such cases, the company depends on its suppliers and cannot play them off against each other.

vii. If there is credible threat of the supplier integrating forward into the industry's business.

viii.When buying companies cannot use the threat of vertically integrating backward and supplying their own needs as a means to reduce input prices.

ix. If the supplier can supply the industry more cheaply than the industry can make the input itself.

x. When the supplier's product significantly affects the quality of the industry's product.

xi. The brand of the supplier is powerful.

In general, suppliers are more likely to exercise their leverage when the competition in their own industry is weak. Some organizations may rely on suppliers other than tangible goods. For example, the provision of finance may be crucial to an organization and therefore, the power of the supplier of finance may be vital.

Human resources also can be a critical area of supply. Professional services such as management consultancy, corporate tax advice, and medicine or teaching, the availability of skilled staff is crucial. If they are not organized, it cannot provide them power. If trade union power is strong, labor supply may exercise power.

In addition to controlling the above factors, the firm can limit the power of the supplier by:

(a) Buying from several sources to insure competition

(b) Dividing orders between suppliers that are themselves in competition;

(c) Occasionally seeking proposals from other suppliers, to collect information and test the market;

(d) Raising the quantities demanded by means of aggregating purchases with sister business units or companies or by making longer term agreements with phased deliveries; or

(e) Attempting to understand the supplier's costs.

Competitive Force # 5. The Threat of Substitute Products:

Substitute products are those products that appear to be different but can satisfy the same need as another product. For example, bottled water is a substitute for a cola. The availability of substitute products influences the actions of the firm's customers.

The fewer are the substitutes, the greater the difficulty of switching to them, the more secure is the firm's revenue. Substitutes limit the potential returns of an industry by placing a ceiling on the prices firms in the industry can profitably charge.

The existence of close substitutes presents a strong competitive threat, limiting the price a company can charge and thus its profitability. For example, tea can be considered a substitute for coffee.

If the price of coffee goes up high enough, coffee drinkers will slowly begin switching to tea. The price of tea thus puts a price cap on the price of coffee. However, if a company's products have few close substitutes, other thing being equal, the company has the opportunity to raise price and earn additional profits.

The threat of substitutes may be actual or potential substitution of one product for another. A new product may render a product superfluous. Substitutes may also be thought of as those competing for discretionary expenditure.

For example, refrigerator manufacturers or retailers should know that they compete for other household expenditure with manufacturers or retailers of television, furniture, video, cookers, gas range, scooter, car etc. 'Doing without' can also be considered as a substitute, as in the case of a tobacco industry.

The strategists also need careful consideration of the strategic impact of actual or potential substitutes.

The availability of substitutes may have the strategic impact on the product or service in the ways:

i. Put a limit on prices of a company's products.

ii. Make dent into the market and so reduce its attractiveness.

iii. Turn a firm's product or service obsolete or provide a higher perceived benefit or value.

However, companies can reduce the risk of substitution by building in switching costs, perhaps through added product or service benefits meeting buyer needs.

Competitive Force # 6. Relative Power of Other Stakeholders:

A sixth force is added to Porter's five forces to include the effect of a variety of stakeholder groups from the task environment. Some of these groups are governments, local communities, creditors, trade associations, special-interest groups, unions, and shareholders. The importance of these stakeholders differs by industry.

Strategic Group Analysis

The companies in an industry might differ with respect to factors, such as use of distribution channels used, serving of market segments, product quality, technological leadership, customer service, pricing policy, advertising policy, and promotions. These differences imply for the opportunities and threats that companies face.

Despite these differences and their implications within most industries, it is possible to observe groups of companies in which each member pursues the same basic strategy as other companies in the group but a strategy different from the one followed by companies in other groups.

These groups of companies are known as strategic groups. A strategic group is a set of business units or firms that "pursue similar strategies with similar resources". The identification of strategic groups within an industry enables the competitive structure of the industry to be redefined to compare strategies of various competitors for similarities and differences and is very useful as a way of better understanding the competitive environment.

Thus some firms may have comparable product lines, be similarly vertically integrated, focus on similar customer segments, use the same distribution channels, sell with the same product positioning, and the like. If all competitors within an industry have similar strategic characteristics, then there will be only one strategic group. However, in most industries with a significant number of competitors it is common for more than one cluster of competitors to emerge.

Strategic group analysis can help build on competitor analysis so as to gain an understanding of the positioning of an organization in relation to the strategies of other organizations.

In a given industry there may be many companies, each of which has different interests and competes on a different basis. In analyzing the relative positions of organizations there is a need for some intermediate level of understanding between that of the individual firm and that of the industry -one such level is the market segment, another is the strategic group.

The purpose of strategic group analysis is to identify clearly defined groupings so that each represents organizations with similar strategic characteristics, following similar strategies or competing on similar bases. Porter argues that such groups can usually be identified using two, or perhaps three, sets of key characteristics.

The strategic group analysis assists better understanding of the degree and nature of competitive rivalry. As a generalization, the closer the strategic groups are to one another, the greater is the likelihood of competitive rivalry between the firms within the group.

Firms that are strategically distant from the main groups may be subject to much less competitive pressure. As a result, the profit potentials of different competitors may be radically different and not necessarily correlated with size. Thus, a large competitor, despite enjoying the advantage of a high market share, may operate within a group in which competitive rivalry is intense, thus leading to profit erosion.

By contrast, a number of competitors operating in a smaller market or strategic space may enjoy superior margins due to the lack of other competitors. Thus competitive pressures will tend to significantly favor some groups over others.

The strategic group analysis is useful in three ways:

1. Helps to gain a better understanding of the bases of rivalry within strategic groups; and also how this is different from that within other groups.

2. Raises the question as to how likely it is for an organization to move from one strategic group to another. Mobility between groups is a matter of considering the extent to which there are barriers to entry between one group and another. Mobility barriers may be substantial, particularly for the multinational groups, but probably also for the own- label producers; the minor national branders are, perhaps, less secure in their position, being susceptible to both major- brand and low- price competition.

3. Strategic groups mapping might also be used to predict market changes or identify strategic opportunities.

Implications of Strategic Group:

Strategic group analysis has a number of implications for industry analysis and the identification of opportunities and threats.

1. A company's immediate competitors are those in its strategic group. Since all the companies in a strategic group are pursuing similar strategies, buyers tend to view the products of such companies as being direct substitutes for each other. Thus a major threat to a company's profitability can come from within its own strategic group.

2. Different strategic groups can have a different standing with respect to the risk of new entry by potential competitors, the degree of rivalry among companies within a group, the bargaining

power of buyers and suppliers, and the competitive force of substitute products and can vary in intensity among different strategic groups within the same industry.

3. Some strategic groups are more desirable than others, for they have a lower level of threats and greater opportunities. Managers must evaluate whether their company would be better off competing in a different strategic group. If the environment of another strategic group is more comfortable, then moving into that group can be regarded as an opportunity.

But the mobility barriers restrict the movement of companies between groups in an industry including both the entry and exit barriers. Thus a company contemplating entry into another strategic group must evaluate the height of mobility barriers before deciding whether the move is worthwhile.

Competitive Intelligence

Strategists do a large part of external environment analysis on an informal and individual basis. Various sources such as suppliers, customers, industry publications, employees, industry experts, industry conferences, and the Internet provide the information for such analysis.

Scientists, engineers and managers working in a firm related to research and development of a firm learn about new products and competitors' ideas at professional meetings; and people from the purchasing department, conversing with supplier-representatives' personnel, may also get important bits of information about a competitor.

A study found that the customer, in the form of inquiries and complaints, initiated 77% of all product innovations in the scientific instruments and 67% in semiconductors and printed circuit boards. In these industries, the sales force and service departments must keep especial vigilance.

Competitive intelligence is a formal program of gathering information on a company's competitors. Until recently, few U.S. corporations had fully developed competitive intelligence programs. In contrast, all Japanese corporations involved in international business and most large European companies have active intelligence programs.

However, the situation is changing now. Competitive intelligence is increasingly getting recognized as one of the fastest growing fields within strategic management. For example, General Mills has trained all its employees to recognize and tap sources of competitive information.

Most companies depend on outside organizations to provide with environmental data.

Hyper Competition

Most industries today are becoming more complex and more dynamic and are facing an ever-increasing level of environmental uncertainty. Industries that remained multi-domestic are going global. New flexible, aggressive, innovative competitors are entering into established markets to erode rapidly the advantages of large previously dominant firms. Distribution channels differ from country to country.

Traditional distribution channels are increasingly giving way to sophisticated information systems. Close relationships with suppliers are proving helpful to reduce costs, increase quality, and gain access to new technology.

It is becoming more difficult to sustain any competitive advantage for a longer period as the companies learn to quickly imitate the successful strategies of market leaders and raising the level of competitive intensity in most industries.

In hyper-competition the frequency, boldness, and aggressiveness of dynamic movement by the players accelerates to create a condition of constant disequilibrium and change. Market stability is threatened by short product life cycles, short product design cycles, new technologies, frequent entry by unexpected outsiders, repositioning by incumbent, and tactical redefinitions of market boundaries as diverse industries merge. In other words, environments escalate toward higher and higher levels of uncertainty, dynamism, heterogeneity of the players and hostility.

In hyper-competitive industries such as computers, competitive advantage flows from an up-to-date knowledge of environmental trends and competitive activity combined with a willingness to risk a short- term advantage for a long term one. Companies must be willing to cannibalize their own products in order to sustain their competitive advantage.

As a result, industry or competitive intelligence has never been more important as they are today. For example, Microsoft, a hyper- competitive firm operating in a hyper-competitive industry has used its dominance in DOS and Windows operating systems to walk into a very strong position in word processing and spreadsheets application programs like Word and Excel.

Even though MS held 90% of the market for PC operating systems in 1992, it still invested hugely in the development of next generation. Instead of trying to protect its advantage in the profitable systems, MS actively sought to replace DOS with various versions of Windows. MS realized that if it did not replace its own product line with a better product, someone else would do.

Formulation of Strategy

Having assessed the forces influencing competition in an industry and their underlying causes, the corporate strategist can identify his company's strengths and weaknesses.

Then the corporate strategist can chalk out a plan of action that may include:

(a) Positioning the company so that its capabilities provide the best defense against the competitive force;

(b) Influencing the balance of forces through strategic moves, thereby improving the company's position; and

(c) Anticipating changes in the factors underlying the forces and responding to them for the purpose of exploiting change by selecting a strategy appropriate for the new competitive balance before competitors recognize it.

In the following paragraphs we discuss these approaches:

Approach # 1. Positioning the Company:

The corporate strategist attempts to match the strengths and weaknesses of the company to its given industry structure. Here, 'strategy can be viewed as building defenses against the competitive forces or as finding positions in the industry where the forces are weakest'. Knowledge of the company's capabilities and the causes of the competitive forces will indicate the areas where the company should face the competition and where to avoid it.

If the company is an efficient one and a low- cost producer, it may decide to face power buyers while taking care to sell them only products not vulnerable to competition from substitutes.

Approach # 2. Influencing the Balance:

When dealing with the forces that drive industry competition, a company can devise a strategy that takes the offensive. This posture is designed to do more than merely cope with the forces themselves; it is meant to alter their causes.

Innovations in marketing can raise brand identification or otherwise differentiate the product. Capital investments in large-scale facilities or vertical integration affect entry barriers. The balance of forces is partly a result of external factors and partly in the company's control.

Approach # 3. Exploiting Industry Change:

From the strategic point of view industry evolution is important because it brings with it changes in the sources of competition. The product life cycle indicates that as a business become more mature the growth rate changes, product differentiation begins to decline and the companies tend to integrate vertically.

These trends are important for the fact that they affect the sources of competition. For example, extensive vertical integration both in manufacturing and in software development in the maturing minicomputer industry is greatly raising economies of scale as well as the amount of capital investment necessary to compete in the industry.

This in turn is raising barriers to entry and may drive some smaller competitors out of the industry once growth levels off. From the strategic point of view, the trends that affect the important sources of competition in the industry and those that bring new causes to the forefront hold the highest priority.

The framework for analyzing competition can also be used to predict the eventual profitability of an industry. For the purpose of long range planning, the strategists have to examine each competitive force, predict the magnitude of each underlying cause, and then construct a composite picture of the likely profit potential of the industry.

The outcome of such an exercise may differ a great deal from the existing industry structure. The framework for analyzing industry competition has direct benefits in setting diversification strategy.

It provides a road map for answering the extremely difficult question relating to potential of a business inherent in diversification decisions. Combining the framework with judgment in its application, a company may be able to spot an industry with a good future before this good future is reflected in the prices of acquisition candidates.

Limitations of Five Forces and Strategic Group Analysis

The five forces and strategic group analysis models provide an understanding of the competitive environment of an industry. However, these models are criticized and mainly two arguments are put forward.

Argument # 1. One argument is that both models present a static picture of competition that diminishes the role of innovation:

In many industries competition can be seen as a process driven by innovation. Companies that innovate products, processes or strategies can earn huge profits. This outlook provides companies a strong motivation to look for innovative products, processes and strategies. The outstanding growth of Apple Computers, Dell Computers, Microsoft or Wal-Mart exemplifies that they all have been innovators.

Successful innovation can revolutionize industry structure. In recent times, it has been experienced that fixed costs of production have reduced because of innovation. This has lowered barriers to entry and allowed new and smaller companies to compete with large established companies.

Once the industry gains stability in its new configuration, the concepts of five forces and strategic groups can once more be applied. This viewpoint of the evolution of industry structure is known as "punctuated equilibrium".

The concept of "punctuated equilibrium" states that long periods of equilibrium characterized by stable industry structure are punctuated by periods of rapid change when innovation revolutionizes industry structure. Thus there is an unfreezing and refreezing process.

However, the industry might gain a new state of equilibrium with a more fragmented or consolidated competitive structure. But the consolidated structure is not common. In general, innovation lowers down barriers to entry resulting entry of more companies into the industry and consequently leads to fragmentation.

Thus five forces and strategic group models apply while the industry is in a stable state but not while it is undergoing radical restructuring due to innovation. They, being static in nature do not take into consideration the factors that change during turbulence, but they are certainly useful for analyzing industry structure during periods of stability.

Argument # 2. Individual Company Differences:

The five forces and strategic group models over-emphasize the importance of industry-structure as a determinant of company performance and be-little the significance of differences between companies within an industry or a strategic group. There can be wide differences in the profit rates of individual companies within an industry.

Rumelt's research suggests that industry structure explains only about 10 percent of the differences in profit rates across companies, while individual company differences explain much of the remainder.

Several other studies suggest that the individual resources and capabilities of a company are far more important determinants of its profitability than is the industry or strategic group of which a company is a member. A company will not be profitable just because it is based in an attractive industry or strategic group.

2.3. Capabilities Analysis as Input to Strategy

A capability map provides visual representation of various capabilities and their performance levels. Only unique capabilities are presented in the organizational capability map. Similar capabilities existing across multiple lines of businesses do not find multiple places in the capability map. Capability analysis should impact value by revenue enhancement or cost reduction or improving service or customer satisfaction or achieving compliance or positioning of the company. Capabilities are assessed for current and expected performance. Gap performance of capability is used as input for strategic planning. This analysis may be done across the organization or within different lines of businesses or units such as sales and marketing, customer service, production, post-delivery support etc. It's important to remember that capabilities do not have any inherent risks, however the non-performance of capabilities do cause risk.

Steps of Capability Based Planning

Because capability-based planning is an approach that impacts all elements of strategic planning and delivery, it is important that organizations embrace all aspects of it.

Define & Communicate Business Capabilities: To begin planning around business capabilities, an organization must first understand those capabilities. That means accurately defining the capabilities, effectively and efficiently communicating with all areas of the business around those capabilities, and ensuring that capabilities are being maintained, matured, and otherwise developed. This is most effectively achieved by leveraging a business architecture approach, including visually mapping current business capabilities.

It's also important to note that business capability mapping cannot be a one-time exercise, capabilities are constantly evolving to meet the needs of the operating environment and customers, to reflect the growing abilities of the enterprise, and to leverage evolving technologies and approaches. Capabilities and associated maps must therefore be maintained, socializing evolving capabilities with all stakeholders, and understanding dependencies and relationships across those capabilities.

Integrate Business Capabilities : Business capabilities don't exist in isolation – the ability to deliver capabilities is based on strategy, organizational value streams, technology, information, people, processes, supply chains, etc. These form both upstream and downstream dependencies for business capabilities and constitute the way that those capabilities are structured and converted to value. Only when all of these aspects and entities are integrated, can the organization fully understand what it does and how it operates, and only then can it successfully evolve through concepts like digital transformation.

The ability to transform a business is critical to sustainable success in today's world. Organizations must be capable of managing their end-to-end strategic capabilities from enterprise architecture models to validating investment performance, and everything in between. That requires skilled enterprise architects developing and maintaining those capabilities and the ability to integrate capability maps and modeling with the entire strategic portfolio management approach of the enterprise. When that is achieved, organizations create a powerful springboard for successful transformation.

Analyze & Model Business Capabilities : Business capability modeling builds on an organization's existing capabilities by mapping potential future state capabilities. That allows for discussion around the need to invest in the development of existing capabilities, to expand into new business functions, or to move away from an element of the current state.

Organizations must be able to combine the capability inventory with user surveys to understand and score capability maturity. This then allows for analysis of current state vs. target state and fuels the development of appropriate strategic objectives and measures that become inputs to strategic planning and investments decisions. In turn, this ensures that the organization's strategic priorities are aligned with the need to enhance and grow business capabilities.

A well-formed and valuable business capability model is so much more than simply the hierarchical capability map. To be of real value, the business capabilities in that map must be cross-related to other elements of the business and enterprise architecture in a consistent manner that allows those cross-relationships to be the "secret sauce" for dynamic, meaningful models, dashboards, and further analysis such as maturity modeling.

Develop Strategic & Technical Roadmaps : Roadmaps provide a powerful way to visualize, collaborate on, and communicate the strategies that will develop and refine business capabilities. Using the right integrated tools, the outputs of the previous analysis work can be developed into roadmaps and rendered as investments - value streams, programs, products, projects, etc. Demand will also come from many other areas of the business, but effective capability-based planning, in conjunction with roadmaps, allows that demand to be assessed in one location, ensuring that all proposed work aligns with the development of business capabilities and the current strategic priorities. This eliminates redundancy and misalignment, while improving return on organizational investments.

Create Detailed Investment Plans : Proposed roadmap investments then require a more comprehensive analysis. Business cases must be developed to allow for effective evaluation of the costs and expected benefits, as well as the way those benefits will be defined and measured. This analysis must consider both financial, and non-financial metrics to ensure the full and accurate picture of expected outcomes is understood. Based on these business cases, decisions can be made to confirm or reconsider investments, and on the scheduling of work. The development and evaluation of these business cases must use the appropriate approach for the type of work being undertaken - formal business cases for more traditional work, or stripped down, lighter analyses for lean portfolio management driven epics. In all cases, capital management software is needed to capture common necessary data points - costs, benefits, milestones, dependencies, resourcing, scoring, etc. to allow for the best possible decision making against the strategic roadmap.

Analyze Funding & Portfolios : Shifting an organization to a business capability-based planning model requires several adjustments. Many organizations already struggle to develop effective strategic planning, running into difficulties with silo-based, bottom-up planning that only nominally aligns with strategic priorities. Effective capability-based planning, and in particular the ability to leverage capability models to enable strategy, requires a commitment to the previously mentioned strategic portfolio management.

Strategic Portfolio Management is increasingly recognized as a more effective approach to strategic planning and delivery. It requires priorities, goals, and objectives to be set by executives - in the case of business capability modeling that will be the business capabilities that are considered the highest priority, and the performance goals that each capability has to deliver. Executives then approve and fund one or more investments for each of those investments, appoint an accountable owner and define success metrics (more on that later).

This top-down approach helps eliminate silos, improve alignment between strategy, work and outcomes, and increase return on investments. Investments must be capable of being prioritized directly from roadmap items, allowing for seamless integration between business capabilities and investments, and providing transparency to all stakeholders on how funded work aligns with strategic priorities.

This approach must evolve to support the organization as it matures. Support for different funding models is important - project level for less mature enterprises, or bulk funding at the investment level for those that are further along their maturity journey. Ultimately, effective capability-based planning requires the ability to derive investments directly from strategy, helping an organization mature to a more comprehensive and effective Strategic Portfolio Management approach to strategy. Detailed analyses of prioritization, optimization, resource capacity planning, fiscal planning, etc. are necessary to help an organization ensure it always makes the right decision based on the best information available.

Deliver Effectively & Perform What-if Analysis: To deliver on your business capabilities you ultimately need to structure and deliver work. That work will be done using any number of different structures and each element of the tri-modal reality. The software solution you use to support your business capability planning must integrate with whatever work management tools teams prefer, consolidating data from multiple sources into a single, value-based, automated status reporting approach. That allows for optimized work delivery while retaining actionable insight across all capabilities and investments. Additionally, there must be the ability to plan continuously and adaptively, so that investment owners can ensure that the work in support of their business capabilities is always optimally aligned with the organization's needs. This also requires dynamic portfolio what-if analysis tools, allowing for easy and rapid analysis of options and impacts should the need to adjust course arise. Only then can decisions be optimized in less time and with less disruption, improving the ability of the organization to maximize ROI even in highly fluid operating environments.

Manage & Realize Benefits: Capability based planning ultimately only benefits the organization if it results in improved capabilities. Benefits realization is an area that organizations have historically struggled with, especially when it comes to non-financial performance metrics. It is essential that organizations can reliably measure performance against strategy aligned metrics easily, and in a timely manner. This allows organizations to understand the improvements being made to the business capabilities that the work supports. Benefits realization software tools must be capable of providing early indicators of areas where performance is deviating from the expected capabilities, driving adjustments more quickly and accurately. Actual performance must feed the capability portfolio, updating current capabilities, and resulting in adjustments to the capability roadmap that then fuel the next cycle of prioritization, investment, and delivery.

Pitfalls to Avoid

Capability based planning isn't a methodology or a set of processes, it's more of a mindset – a way of thinking about the business. As a result, most of the pitfalls around the concept are around a lack of understanding and misinterpreting what business capabilities really are.

Organizations shouldn't view business capability maps, or even capability-based planning in isolation. It requires an understanding of enterprise architecture and the related discipline of business architecture. Without this, there are likely to be problems in defining and mapping capabilities, often resulting in a focus on functions and processes rather than capabilities.

Similarly, to optimize capability-based planning, organizations must be willing to embrace a value stream management approach. Value streams represent a series of activities that combine to deliver customer value, enabling business capabilities in the process. Combining business capabilities with value streams helps organizations optimize performance.

Modeling vs Planning

But simply understanding capabilities and modeling possible futures isn't enough. Organizations must also execute to create those capabilities. Capability based planning helps ensure that all resources - people and financial - are used optimally to support those capabilities. This happens through approval and delivery of the right investments and the right work, delivered through effective strategy execution management. Capability based planning then becomes an enabler of further business transformation, supporting an organization's ability to evolve and grow by ensuring that the focus is always on optimizing the ability to deliver what matters to organizations and their customers. At the same time, it helps prevent the dilution of strategic plans through the approval of tactical, bottom-up initiatives that don't align with those capabilities, and don't move the organization forward.

2.4. Competitive Advantage

Competitive advantage refers to factors that allow a company to produce goods or services better or more cheaply than its rivals. These factors allow the productive entity to generate more sales or superior margins compared to its market rivals. Competitive advantages are attributed to a variety of factors including cost structure, branding, the quality of product offerings, the distribution network, intellectual property, and customer service.

Understanding Competitive Advantage

Competitive advantages generate greater value for a firm and its shareholders because of certain strengths or conditions. The more sustainable the competitive advantage, the more difficult it is for competitors to neutralize the advantage. The two main types of competitive advantages are comparative advantage and differential advantage. A comparative advantage is when a firm can produce products more efficiently and at a lower cost than its competitors. A differential advantage is when a firm's products or services differ from its competitors' offerings and are seen as superior. Advanced technology, patent-protected products or processes, superior personnel, and strong brand identity are all drivers of differential advantage. These factors support wide margins and large market shares. Competing on price can be effective, but if you slash prices too much you risk decreasing profit margins to an untenable level. Many firms opt instead to differentiate themselves in other ways, which helps preserve or expand their profit margin.

Competitive Advantage Areas

To build a competitive advantage, a company can use one of three main methods:

- **Cost:** Provide offerings at the lowest price
- **Differentiation:** Provide offerings that are superior in quality, service, or features
- **Specialization:** Provide offerings narrowly tailored to a focused market

How to Build a Competitive Advantage

To build a competitive advantage, a company must know what sets it apart from its competitors and then focus its message, service, and products with that difference in mind. Here are several strategies companies use to build a competitive advantage:

- **Research the market**: Market research helps a company identify and define its target market, which can guide it in developing the most effective advantage.
- **Identify strengths**: A company can find its unique strengths, especially relative to competitors, by reviewing products, services, features, positioning, and branding.
- **Evaluate finances**: Companies can take a close look at their financial performance to spot profit centers and areas of stability, using financial statements and ratios.
- **Review operations**: How efficient is a company's operations? Where is it effective, and where is there room for improvement? Consider customer service as well as production and supply chain management.
- **Research and development (R&D):** Securing intellectual property prohibits competitors from using processes or know-how that the company can use to produce products competitors can't legally copy.
- **Consider human resources**: The talent a company can attract as employees and leadership can make an important difference in the success of the business. Evaluating company culture, hiring, and staffing practices can help.

Competitive Advantage vs. Comparative Advantage

A firm's ability to produce a good or service more efficiently than its competitors, which leads to greater profit margins, creates a comparative advantage. Rational consumers will choose the cheaper of any two perfect substitutes offered. For example, a car owner will buy gasoline from a gas station that is 0.5 paise cheaper than other stations in the area. For imperfect substitutes, like Pepsi versus Coke, higher margins for the lowest-cost producers can eventually bring superior returns. Economies of scale, efficient internal systems, and geographic location can also create a comparative advantage.

Components of Competitive Advantage

For a competitive advantage to be established, it is important to know the following:

1. **Value proposition:** A company must clearly identify the features or services that make it attractive to customers. It must offer real value in order to generate interest.

2. **Target market:** A company must establish its target market to further engrain best practices that will maintain competitiveness.

3. **Competitors:** A company must define competitors in the marketplace, and research the value they offer; this includes both traditional as well as non-traditional, emerging competition.

To build a competitive advantage, a company must be able to identify its value proposition that will be sought after by the target market, which cannot be replicated by competitors.

Protecting the Competitive Advantage

The company that holds the advantage tends to maintain this position (in certain cases it can exploit a monopolistic position), whereas competitors tend to erode (destroy) the advantage. The erosion of the advantage can take place either through imitation or creation of a new advantage.

Therefore, whereas the holder of the advantage has to defend its competitive advantage, the competitors have to erode (destroy) this advantage. The time window in which the competitive advantage can be held over competitors brings to the concept of the sustainability of the advantage: the larger time window, the more sustainable advantage. The sustainability is related to the capability/opportunity to protect the firm's source of advantage. Factors of protection are the following.

Secrecy. It is a form of protection especially if the source of competitive advantage is the production process. Although information can be obtained from products and there is an inevitable leakage of know-how through a variety of channels (technical community, suppliers, etc.), firms can keep secrecy over that. Firms that do not open their plants to anyone external to the firm may succeed in keeping their own process innovations secret.

Accumulated tacit knowledge. If the knowledge at the basis of the advantage is strongly embodied into people and technical systems, and relies upon people's experience, it is difficult to make the knowledge explicit, and the related advantage can be highly protected. The well-known case of Italian small firms, often world leaders in niche markets and traditional manufacturing industries, is largely based on the accumulation of tacit knowledge. In very concentrated geographical areas (districts), there are networks of small firms that are strongly specialized in highly specific manufactures. Knowledge is, to a large extent, embedded in people living in that area.

Lead times. The ability to generate and quickly put new products on the market is a major source of advantage and is itself a major source of protection against imitation. It helps establish brand loyalty and credibility, accelerate feedback from customer use, accelerate learning effects, and consequently increase cost of entry for imitators. The market leadership is based on the ability to provide new generations of products frequently and stay ahead of competitors.

Complementary assets. The ability to make profits from the commercialization of a new product or service often depends on the availability of assets or competencies, such as production capabilities, marketing, distribution, after-sale service, which are complementary to the product and its technology. These complementary assets determine who exploits the new product introduction and the appropriation of the related benefits and to what extent. As a matter of fact, they are often the reason for failures of firms, that, having once generated the new product do not have the required complementary assets to exploit it or have to invest largely to acquire them. Both these conditions may cause the firm not to create a competitive advantage from the new product introduction. On the other hand, the availability of complementary assets for the firm may represent not only the means which ensure that profits are made from new product introduction but also a barrier against imitation by competitors especially when such assets may be difficult to acquire, access, or imitate.

Product complexity. In some sectors, product complexity is a major barrier against imitators. The large electromechanical equipment industry or the aircraft industry is a typical example.

Standards. In certain industries, making the firm's own product accepted as a standard opens and develops the market and raises barriers against competitors. This is especially true in network markets, where the compatibility of a product with related products (for example a software package with the related hardware) is a prerequisite for the product's success. Once the product is diffused throughout the market as a standard, it is difficult for competitors to erode the advantage. In fact, new products marketed by competitors should replace the existing product but may also involve the replacement of the other related products. This represents a major barrier. Computing, telecommunication, consumer electronics industries show examples in which standard setting is a key factor to appropriate the benefits of new product introduction and create a sustainable competitive advantage.

Pioneering radical new products. If a product is radically new, i.e., represents a strong discontinuity with the existing products/processes/services and lies upon a base of knowledge that is completely different from that behind traditional products, the firm is more protected against imitation. Potential imitators cannot rely on the existing knowledge base to replicate the product.

Strength of patent protection. Patenting is also a major means of protection. This is especially true in some sectors, chemical and pharmaceutical for example, where products can be clearly and rigorously described (often with a structural formula) and imitation by small differences is not easy as in most industries.

2.5. Execute Strategy through Business Models

Strategy execution has become a hot topic within management. It is estimated that over 60% of strategies are not successfully implemented. Senior executives have revealed that effective strategy execution is one of their most challenging matters. If you've ever tried to execute a strategy, chances are you agree with this statement. If you ask your manager what he thinks Strategy Execution is, he'll probably answer something like "the successful implementation of a plan" or "follow through with your strategy". These statements might be somewhat true, but it doesn't really tell us everything that strategy execution entails and how to successfully do it to drive top results. A more proper definition would be "strategy execution is translating an organization's strategic initiatives into action". It is the crucial step after a long planning process, and it is extremely important to do it right not just to make the planning process worth it, but to obtain the best outcomes.

The foundations of execution

Strategic definition is not enough. A systematic approach is required to get the ball rolling on your primary objectives. This is what this post is about. Once you've defined your value proposition, you must ensure that all the pieces are in place in order to bring that vision to life.

It starts out with an honest assessment of what your resources and capabilities are and more importantly, what resources and capabilities you need. In the case of a business these include, capital, assets, brands, technologies, organizational design and culture, relationships, etc.

The first approach, and a rather simplistic one, would have you select the resources & capabilities where the company is better than the competition, and do your best to strengthen and expand them. These can be leveraged to diversify the product/service offering. This would be the case with Apple, whose innovation capabilities, have allowed them to constantly add products to their portfolio. Started out with the Mac, the iPod, iPad, iPhone, iTunes and so on. On the other hand, those resources & capabilities where one is weaker or at a disadvantage vs the competition, should be outsourced. Common outsourced services include staffing, back office services such as accounting and payroll. There are other less evident options as well. Consider Microsoft. They outsource jobs such as software architect or software testing engineers. The key point is whether internal capacities are efficiently above competitors'. If not, outsourcing should be seriously considered. This rather straightforward concept alone should increase your odds of achieving your strategic objectives. It creates focus within the organization.

The second approach, if you're up for a little more ambitious endeavor, would have you reverse engineer those strategic objectives and build a resource & capabilities staircase to track over time, all the while aimed at creating a sustainable competitive advantage. This would be a more comprehensive program that builds on itselt by implementing specific development programs, in specific time frames.

An example best illustrates the concept. Take a company like Coca Cola. It has recently stated its intent on becoming "a total beverage company". That requires focus indeed. First on the list, refranchising of company-owned bottling operations. Local partners are simply more efficient at this particular task. They have better resources & capabilities, so it is outsourced.

What about the resources & capabilities that are kept inhouse? Those at which Coca Cola excels. There's a few key elements to consider. Coca Cola's value proposition is built around an iconic brand, with cultural appeal and an emotional connection.

The graph illustrates some of the core resources & capabilities Coca Cola has developed over time. You'll notice it looks like a staircase. A resources & capabilities staircase. The analogy fits well, for a strong base provides the necessary support to keep adding capacity (in this case more resources and more capabilities) to its foundation.

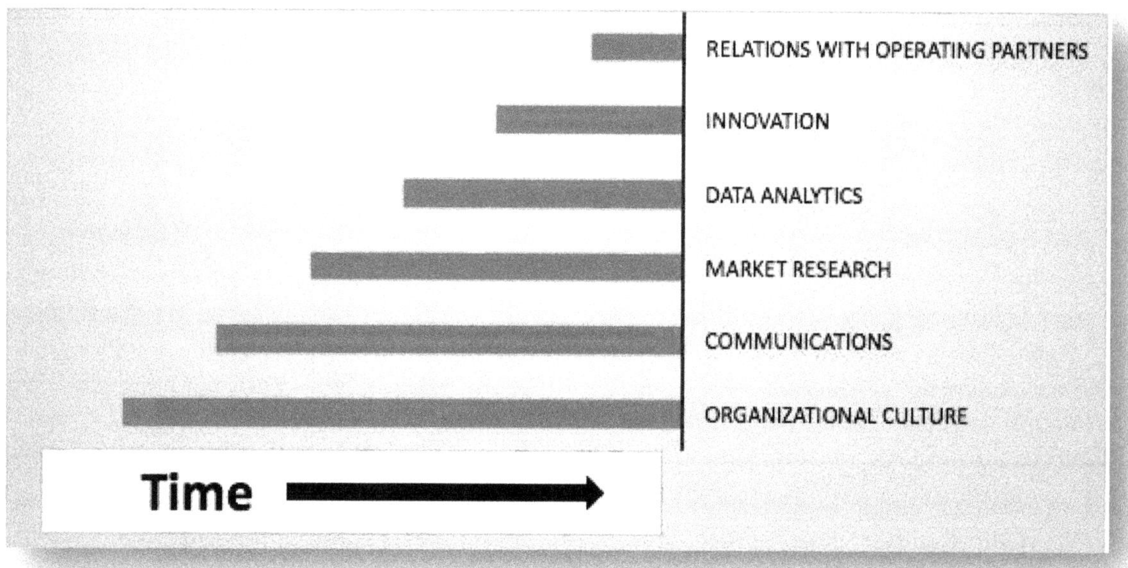

The greatest companies build on top of that which they have already developed. In this illustrative example, it all begins with a great organizational culture. After that a communications capability is developed that values honest, transparent communication with all stakeholders. From their communications with customers a great market research program is implemented, and through the use of data analytics, the most valuable insights are generated that allow the company to keep on innovating and keeping up with market trends. In this case, Coca Cola is lowering their sugar content and constantly introducing alternatives for a healthier lifestyle. All this eventually facilitates maintaining good working relations with their operating partners, for risk and reward are shared.

The result of this staircase is a learning and development system that enables the company to create and maintain its most precious asset by achieving their strategic objectives.

Why is Strategy Execution Important?

To sum it up, big corporations and leaders spend hundreds of hours and dollars on strategic initiatives that are often not executed as intended. This can deprive customers of innovative technology or service if a company fails to execute a marketing or selling strategy to its target customers. In the end, no matter how amazingly brilliant a strategy looks on paper, it can only shine when put into action in everyday activities.

Research indicates that over 80% of strategies fail. And they fail not because they're incorrect, they fail because they're not correctly executed. Day-to-day as people do their daily work, this work is not aligned to the Strategic objectives or priorities. This results in a considerable waste of effort and resources as people from across the organization work in opposition to two other activities. A successful company relies not only on its managers' shoulders, but also on their teams'; every employee no matter their position or hierarchy has an important role to play, and if one piece is not properly executing their job, the whole strategy could fail.

Dissecting a Strategy

It can be difficult to change your employees' mindset from a fully operational framework to a strategic execution framework and getting everyone involved in what the whole company needs and how they fit into those needs. Effective and successful strategy execution requires that their employees have discipline, and this is achieved through setting detailed and doable tasks to move the company strategy from paper into action. To achieve strategic goals, a strategy needs to be created through a strategic plan that can be followed.

Creation of the Strategy

Many companies struggle with growth because their strategies are based on wrong assumptions regarding what customers want, what their teams are capable of, or what the competition is doing. Not having clear information to plan the strategy will eventually result in bumps in the road that will only delay the execution and prevent the strategy's success. When creating your strategy, it's important to test different scenarios, using mechanisms to identify and challenge strategic assumptions to get ahead of whatever issues are possible to appear and prevent implementation.

Strategic Planning

Often organizations hold strategic planning meetings spending hundreds of hours, and therefore, money. But all of these efforts can go to waste when there are not clear strategic goals and target alignment throughout the organization, preventing a successful execution of the organizational strategy that took so many hours to plan. Do not miss the main focus during the strategic planning process, choose a vertical alignment going through corporate and business units, and choose a horizontal alignment across business units and operational ones. When discussing the strategy with your teams, be specific regarding the objectives and roles for everyone in each business unit. Keep in mind that every hour held to the strategy development should be put to good use, so leave no room for confusion. It takes way less time to get aligned than it costs not to be; each quarter people have 530 hours to contribute to victory, and it takes about 5 hours to set proper OKRs that maximize their contribution.

How to Execute a Strategy Successfully?

Yes, everyone is a key piece when it's time to execute a strategy, but it is up to the corporate leaders to verify everything is going according to plan; and this strategic plan could sometimes shift depending on the ever-changing markets. We cannot always predict how the market is going to react or respond to different situations, but we can anticipate ourselves with backup strategies and preparing our senior leaders to face these emerging threats and not waste precious time working on a strategic plan that's bound to fail eventually. The techniques listed below are intended to help managers understand the complexities of strategy implementation and to provide guidance on the aspects that will help companies achieve a successful strategy execution.

Ensure that plans are aligned with the organizational mission, vision, and core values
If your organization's strategies exhibit behaviors that are in conflict with your values, you will see a gradual degradation in your this team and engagement, as your employees see that you are "just kidding" around your core values.

Build an effective leadership team: Determine your team's work strictly in terms of its end goal - what is the outcome this team is chartered to deliver? Once we've determined where we are going to drive the bus (what the goals are for this team) we can then sort out who are the best people on the bus to sit in which seats (who should be playing what roles in the team in order to drive maximum effectiveness).

Create an implementation plan: Setting your team's implementation plan depends on the people that make up the team, play to their strengths, and set OKRs with realistic deadlines. Have frequent meetings to analyze whether the implementation of the strategy is going according to plan or if there is a need to make changes.

Allocate budgetary resources: It's common for companies to try to execute a strategy working their way around budgeting, and even though it's important not to splurge, don't be afraid to allocate the monetary resources when needed. You could end up spending more money making up for the mistake of not budgeting from the beginning.

Assign objectives and responsibilities: This may sound self-explanatory but keep in mind that sometimes we think some responsibilities and objectives are intended within others, but remember you can't leave any grey areas when executing a strategy.

Align structures and end-to-end processes: Without the alignment of end-to-end processes, you risk customer satisfaction. If your organization is structured as functional silos with little interaction, you're likely to buy or build different systems for each department that also communicate poorly. Maintain communication to align structures throughout the organization and find success from start to finish.

Align people: Aligning your people starts from your company's core values all the way up to their goals and tasks. Without a strong foundation, you won't be able to align everyone towards a common benefit.

Communicate the strategy: As obvious as it sounds, you can't expect your team to execute a strategy successfully if it's not well communicated. We'll go deeper into this point later in the article.

Review and report on progress: Make sure to set weekly or biweekly meetings with your team to review progress and make thorough reports. This is the only way to make sure your strategy is on its way to success and to fix whatever challenges come your way.

Make strategic adjustments as necessary: Don't be afraid to re-strategize. Even if your team is performing well, there can be outside factors that can negatively affect your implementation of the strategy. Every time you review your progress, analyze if you should make adjustments.

Develop an organizational culture that supports the strategy: The culture of a company is the backbone of every process and department, it defines the personality of your organization and represents your values. This backbone needs to support not only your organization but the way to execute your strategies.

Having a system to monitor the performance and development of the company's strategy is a key element for successful strategy execution and achieving strategic goals. When assigning your employees OKRs and/or KPIs, hold them accountable and ask them to keep you updated on their performance. Using a project and performance management dashboard can determine if underperformance is the result of a shift in the market, a misleading strategy, or simply poor execution from your team.

Communication

A lot of the problems companies face today revolves around a lack of communication. Sometimes we aren't clear enough, sometimes we are afraid to ask questions or have a hard time admitting we don't fully understand what we have to do and just wing it expecting the best results which obviously don't work out. But the truth is that to execute a good strategy, its implementation completely depends on a 100% understanding (and supporting) of such strategy. Still,

Behind a successful strategy implementation lies an effective communication strategy, one that motivates employees to thrive and avoids resistance from employees to perform satisfactorily. Employee Engagement plays a huge part here. Remember that engaged employees transmit motivation to their peers, and an employee committed to a specific business strategy can get more support towards it from other employees. Maintain a two-way communication channel between key managers and employees to continue motivating and engaging employees in order to achieve the company's strategic goals.

Organizational Resources

Unfortunately, it's common to see many companies failing to allocate resources strategically for the implementation of strategies. A common mistake is to heavily rely on the creation of the business strategy, planning, and OKRs and KPIs implementation. But what about the loopholes? Research shows that There's always one or more areas where the performance is poor or there's a lack of coordination on a strategic plan. The result of poor coordination is a substantial reduction in the overall capacity of the organization, and this is becoming quite an issue. An increase in the cross-organizational dialogue and careful communication between departments can thoroughly help identify these deficiencies and conflicts before they happen.

Addressing Efforts

There are four areas organizations need to address to easily improve the likelihood of a successful strategy execution:

1. Accurately cascade the strategy down the organization and/or build the strategy up from the grassroots. This is not the ongoing debate about whether the strategy should be talked down or bottom-up, but rather the need to ensure strategic alignment whether it is established from the top-down, or bottom-up.

What we see frequently is a strategy set at the top, such as "enter new markets with our existing products" gets restated and restated and restated as it's cascaded down the organization, and by the time it is reviewed at the front line that same strategy is articulated as "grow our existing markets with new products".

This is reminiscent of the child game "broken telephone", whereas a story gets repeated from child to child and it gradually changes, until it ends up being something either somewhat or entirely different.

2. Clearly setting corporate priorities. Not all of the organization's strategic objectives are equally important. It is critical that the organization understands which objectives are more important. Moment-to-moment departments, teams and employees are making strategic decisions between doing activity 'A' and activity 'B' without the proper framework to make an informed decision. Again, the output here is misalignment across the organization and employees working in opposition to each other.

It is also important to note that these strategic priorities shift over time. Back when many of the foundational business books and practices were established, for example in the 1960s with Peter Drucker, a philosophy of annual strategic planning was established. With the current pace of business and business turbulence, we feel that in many cases even a quarterly strategy update is too infrequent. The COVID lockdowns of 2020 are a classic example where annual or even quarterly strategic refreshes are too infrequent.

3. Strategic goals and objectives need clear owners to ensure success. People need to know what they're accountable for, and even the type of accountability they have. This is where Concepts like RACI and RAPID allow for clear role clarity and responsibilities. Frameworks that ensure all of us work the right way on the right tasks.

4. Establishing a learning organization. Someone once said, "every strategic battle plan fails on first contact with the Enemy" (not the exact quote from Helmuth von Moltke the Elder). The same happens in your organization. Day to day as the markets change, your product development process moves forward (or not), competitors enter and leave the market, etc., the plans you made at the beginning of the year quickly get outdated by day-to-day events.

It is critical that you build into your organization the ability to quickly gather data, put it into strategic contact, learn from what is recorded, and act with agility in response. This practice of agile management will differentiate the winners from the losers.

The best tools and frameworks for executing your strategy effectively

OKR: One of the most widely used models for strategy execution is OKR, which stands for Objectives and Key Results. OKR is a simple and flexible framework that helps you define and communicate your strategic priorities, measure your outcomes, and align your teams and stakeholders. The basic idea is to set a few ambitious and inspiring objectives for each quarter or year, and then break them down into specific and measurable key results that indicate how well you are achieving them. OKR helps you focus on the most important goals, track your performance, and foster a culture of transparency and accountability.

Balanced Scorecard: Another popular model for strategy execution is the Balanced Scorecard, which is a comprehensive and holistic framework that helps you translate your vision and mission into four perspectives: financial, customer, internal, and learning and growth. The Balanced Scorecard helps you identify and monitor the key indicators that reflect your strategic objectives, as well as the initiatives and actions that support them. The Balanced Scorecard helps you balance your short-term and long-term goals, align your activities with your strategy, and improve your organizational learning and innovation.

Hoshin Kanri: A third model for strategy execution is Hoshin Kanri, which is a Japanese term that means "direction management" or "policy deployment". Hoshin Kanri is a systematic and collaborative approach that helps you align your strategic goals with your operational plans, and ensure that everyone in your organization is working towards the same vision. The core elements of Hoshin Kanri are the catchball process, which is a dialogue between different levels of management and employees to agree on the goals and actions, and the PDCA cycle, which is a continuous improvement method that involves planning, doing, checking, and acting.

Agile: A fourth model for strategy execution is Agile, which is a flexible and adaptive framework that helps you respond to changing customer needs, market conditions, and technological opportunities. Agile is based on the principles of delivering value quickly and frequently, collaborating with customers and stakeholders, empowering self-organizing teams, and embracing feedback and learning. Agile helps you execute your strategy in an iterative and incremental way, using short cycles of work called sprints, and using tools such as user stories, backlogs, and retrospectives.

Strategy Map: A fifth model for strategy execution is the Strategy Map, which is a visual tool that helps you communicate and align your strategic objectives across your organization. A Strategy Map is a diagram that shows how your different goals are linked and support each other, and how they contribute to your overall vision and mission. A Strategy Map helps you clarify and communicate your strategy, identify and prioritize your initiatives, and align your resources and capabilities.

The Best Framework for Effective Strategy Execution

Most Executives and Managers would agree that the successful execution of strategy remains one of the biggest challenges for organisations. Most organisations therefore consider that executing strategy goes beyond doling out templates and frameworks (such as the Balanced Scorecard or Objectives & Key Results) which are only as useful as the strategy and effort backing them up. In the past ten years of working with several Teams and Organisations in driving Strategy execution, one thing I have found helpful in addition to defining what winning means for the organisation, is to evaluate the "how do we win" of the strategy to ensure it can deliver the strategy promise before coming up with concrete plans.

What this means is that;

1. All the key stakeholders required to drive home the strategy are duly involved in the strategy crafting (i.e set of choices that can help the organisation deliver unique value in a way that It wins the mind and pockets of It's target customers) and their perspectives are captured in arriving at the goals and targets. This will not only get their buy-in but ensure we are setting realistic & achievable goals.

2. In setting realistic goals and targets, the company must ensure it has the capabilities and competencies required to achieve the strategy or at least a SMART way of closing such gaps either through training, partnership, outsourcing, hiring or head-hunting.

3. Although separate from Business As Usual, the strategy should be woven into the fabric of everyday work life. It must be transitioned from the big-picture strategy to daily actionable tasks. This implies that the daily activities of each Responsibility Owner should not be different from the daily plans required to reach the company's aspiration of delivering a unique value proposition that solves the problem of Its target customers. It also requires that all Responsibility Owners are clear on what their role is in the whole strategy big picture and they are equipped with the requisite tools and resources to fulfil their roles.

4. Promotions and rewards must be in sync with the achievement of goals and targets that help deliver on the strategy as assigned to each Responsibility Owner. Consequently, there should be constant measurement (daily/weekly/biweekly/monthly/quarterly/biannually/annually), monitoring and evaluation of these goals and targets. This should serve as a form of check and balance to steer everyone in the same direction towards the agreed expected end.

5. Finally, change is unavoidable. Therefore, there must be a clear path and standard for accommodating change as it affects the definition of winning for the organisation and the set of choices that facilitates this. This ensures that beyond any framework, the strategy remains a living document that takes cognisance of the realities of our industry, markets, competition, regulatory & policy environment, unforeseen contingencies, etc.

In a nutshell, whereas frameworks are useful and recommended, executing strategy is not and should not be a rote job that is constrained by a framework. It should be an active exercise that duly captures the choices, SMART aspirations and peculiarities of the organisation, its markets, key external factors and stakeholders in a way that assures winning. This way, we can avoid ramming down unrealistic goals down people's throat in the hopes that a framework will ease its absorption. We should strive to always "begin with the end in mind".

2.6. Strategies for Growth

Every business faces the existential threat of competitors. Many small businesses don't make it to the ten-year mark. For this reason, you have to be strategic from the very start as a small business owner. If you don't have a tangible development strategy for your business, you risk losing business to your competitors and even obsoletion. What's the one thing you can do to ensure your small business is sustainable? A growth strategy is a clear, actionable plan that will set your business on the path to long-term success. It's a plan that makes your position in the market more dominant and stable while capitalizing on opportunities for market expansion. What's more, you may run a small business now, but that may not always be the case. Inevitably, you'll need the help of small business advisory services to develop a growth strategy that orients your company towards success and ensures the sustainable expansion of your business. There are four major business growth strategies that will ensure growth and profitability go hand in hand for your company.

Increase Market Penetration : A market penetration strategy aims to increase the sales of your products or services within your current market. Pricing is one of the main tactics companies use to grow their share of the market while increasing revenues. Lowering prices and bundling product offerings work well in gaining traction in market portions you haven't yet penetrated. As a small business owner, it may not always be practical to charge considerably lower rates for your offerings. Lowering prices typically work when costs can be spread over a larger number of goods. As such, it's important to work with a small business advisor to determine which market expansion strategies will work best for you. Some strategies employ social media campaigns, direct sales outreach, and other marketing strategies to reach untapped market segments.

Product Development and Diversification: There's a reason why Apple releases a new iPhone every year – to keep customers coming back to buy the newest release. Improving existing products is an efficient yet cost-effective method for product development since you don't have to dedicate a lot of time and resources to creating a new product. A well-designed product development strategy can breathe new life into your business, helping your brand stay relevant with its customer base while naturally growing your market share. Similarly, market conditions evolve with time, as do consumer preferences, so it makes sense to adjust your product mix accordingly. As a business growth strategy, product development helps you keep pace with changing technologies, trends, and preferences, while diversification opens up new markets for your business.

Strategic Partnerships and Acquisitions: In this strategy, you can grow your market share by collaborating with complementary businesses. Partnering with another small business will give your company access to its existing audience. Ideally, the partnership ought to benefit both businesses significantly. It can involve developing a new product that serves the interests of both parties or hosting an event to promote both brands. Acquisition is another business growth strategy that can increase your market share. It involves buying a large portion of another company to gain control of its operations. The principal motive for acquisitions is to create value, whether by increasing economies of scale, business diversification, or increasing market power. Strategic partnerships and acquisitions require a great deal of market research. A business advisory firm will provide you with the data and tools needed to make the right decision.

Market Development: Market development is a business growth strategy aimed at capturing an entirely new market share. Small businesses often struggle to gain a footing in competitive markets because they don't have the same resources as larger brands. That's why it's important to evaluate your company's market position and narrow down your target. Every market can be divided into smaller subsets based on factors such as demographic characteristics or buying habits. Focusing on a specific market segment like underserved or unserved demographics, can help you expand your business. Plus, creating a marketing strategy that appeals to a specific group of potential customers is far easier than trying to appeal to a massive group.

Chapter 3: Business Model Innovation

Business model innovation is fundamental to competitive value in the new economy. The learnings from this course will enable you to reinvigorate growth for your firm through a deeper understanding of your current business model, whether it enables or hinders the pursuit of new market opportunities, especially in the digital economy, and pathways to building new business models.

3.1 An Introduction to Business Models

The term business model refers to a company's plan for making a profit. It identifies the products or services the business plans to sell, its identified target market, and any anticipated expenses. Business models are important for both new and established businesses. They help companies attract investment, recruit talent, and motivate management and staff. Businesses should regularly update their business model or they'll fail to anticipate trends and challenges ahead. Business models also help investors to evaluate companies that interest them and employees to understand the future of a company they may aspire to join.

A business model is a high-level plan for profitably operating a business in a specific marketplace. This plan helps the company to identify the best way to go about doing its business while also serving to attract investors and talent. A primary component of the business model is the value proposition. This is a description of the goods or services that a company offers and why they are desirable to customers or clients; it should ideally be stated in a way that differentiates the product or service from its competitors. A new enterprise's business model should also cover projected startup costs and financing sources, the target customer base for the business, marketing strategy, a review of the competition, and projections of revenues and expenses. The plan may also define opportunities in which the business can partner with other established companies. For example, the business model for an advertising business may identify benefits from an arrangement for referrals to and from a printing company. Successful businesses have business models that allow them to fulfill client needs at a competitive price and a sustainable cost. And they are subject to change. Many businesses revise their business models periodically to reflect changing business environments and market demand.

Investors and Business Models

When evaluating a company as a possible investment, the investor should find out exactly how it makes its money. This means looking through the company's business model. Fortunately, it's not hard to find. Most companies outline their business model on their website and in their annual reports. Admittedly, the business model may not tell you everything about a company's prospects. Investors need to fill in the blanks, look beyond the sales pitch, and recognize that sensitive information or any flouting of rules of ethics to gain an advantage won't be mentioned. The investor who understands the business model, even on a basic level, can make better sense of the financial data.

Evaluating Successful Business Models

A common mistake many companies make when they create their business models is to underestimate the costs of funding the business until it becomes profitable. Counting costs up to the introduction of a product is not enough. A company has to keep the business running until its revenues exceed its expenses.

One way analysts and investors evaluate the success of a business model is by looking at the company's gross profit. Gross profit is a company's total revenue minus the cost of goods sold (COGS). Comparing a company's gross profit to that of its main competitor or its industry sheds light on the efficiency and effectiveness of its business model. Gross profit alone can be misleading, however. Analysts also want to see cash flow or net income—that is, gross profit minus operating expenses, which is an indication of just how much real profit the business is generating.

The two primary levers of a company's business model are pricing and costs. A company can raise prices, and it can find inventory at reduced costs. Both actions increase gross profit.

Many analysts consider gross profit to be more important in evaluating a business plan. A good gross profit suggests a sound business plan. In that case, if expenses are out of control, the management team could be at fault, and the problems are correctable. As this suggests, many analysts believe that companies that run on the best business models can run themselves.

Types of Business Models

There isn't one type of business model. Not all companies are the same and each has different ways of making money. Business models can vary considerably. An aerospace company such as Boeing, for example, may operate similarly to a peer such as Airbus but won't share much in common in terms of how it makes money with, say, a shoe store or bar.

Direct sales, franchising, advertising-based, and brick-and-mortar stores are all examples of traditional business models. There are hybrid models as well, such as businesses that combine internet retail with brick-and-mortar stores or with sporting organizations.

Below are some common types of business models; note that the examples given may fall into multiple categories.

Retailer: One of the more common business models most people interact with regularly is the retailer_model. A retailer is the last entity along a supply chain. They often buy finished goods from manufacturers or distributors and interface directly with customers.

Manufacturer: Is responsible for sourcing raw materials and producing finished products by leveraging internal labor, machinery, and equipment. A manufacturer may make custom goods or highly replicated, mass-produced products and can sell what it makes to distributors, retailers, or directly to customers.

Fee-for-Service: Instead of selling products, fee-for-service business models are centered around labor and providing services. A fee-for-service business model may charge an hourly rate or a fixed cost for a specific agreement. Fee-for-service companies are often specialized, offering insight that may not be common knowledge or may require specific training.

Subscription: Subscription-based business models strive to attract clients in the hopes of luring them into long-time, loyal patrons. This is done by offering a product that requires ongoing payment, usually in return for a fixed duration of benefit. Though largely offered by digital companies for access to software, subscription business models are also popular for physical goods such as monthly reoccurring agriculture/produce subscription box deliveries.

Freemium: Business models attract customers by introducing them to basic, limited-scope products. Then, with the client using their service, the company attempts to convert them to a more premium, advance product that requires payment. Although a customer may theoretically stay on freemium forever, a company tries to show the benefit of becoming an upgraded member.

Bundling: If a company is concerned about the cost of attracting a single customer, it may attempt to bundle products to sell multiple goods to a single client. Bundling capitalizes on existing customers by attempting to sell them different products. This can be incentivized by offering pricing discounts for buying multiple products.

Marketplace: Marketplaces receive compensation for hosting a platform for business to be conducted. Although transactions could occur without a marketplace, this business model attempts to make transacting easier, safer, and faster.

Affiliate: Affiliate business models are based on marketing and the broad reach of a specific entity or person's platform. Companies pay an entity to promote a good, and that entity often receives compensation in exchange for their promotion. That compensation may be a fixed payment, a percentage of sales derived from their promotion, or both.

Razor Blade: Aptly named after the product that invented the model, this business model aims to sell a durable product below cost to then generate high-margin sales of a disposable component needed to use that product. Also referred to as the "razor and blade model", razor blade companies may give away expensive blade handles with the premise that consumers need to continually buy razor blades in the long run.

Reverse Razor Blade: Instead of relying on high-margin companion products, a reverse razor blade business model tries to sell a high-margin product upfront. Then, to use the product, low or free companion products are provided. This model aims to promote that upfront sale, as further use of the product is not highly profitable.

Franchise: The franchise business model leverages existing business plans to expand and reproduce a company at a different location. Often food, hardware, or fitness companies, franchisers work with incoming franchisees to finance the business, promote the new location, and oversee operations. In return, the franchisor receives a percentage of earnings from the franchisee.

Pay-As-You-Go: Instead of charging a fixed fee, some companies may implement a pay-as-you-go business model where the amount charged depends on how much of the product or service was used. The company may charge a fixed fee for offering the service in addition to an amount that changes each month based on what was consumed.

Brokerage: A brokerage business model connects buyers and sellers without directly selling a good themselves. Brokerage companies often receive a percentage of the amount paid when a deal is finalized. Most common in real estate, brokers are also prominent in construction/development and freight.

How to Create a Business Model

There is no "one size fits all" when making a business model. Different professionals may suggest taking different steps when creating a business and planning your business model. Here are some broad steps someone can take to create a plan:

1. **Identify your audience**: Most business model plans will start with either defining the problem or identifying your audience and target market. A strong business model will reflect who you are trying to target so you can craft your product, messaging, and approach to connecting with that audience.

2. **Define the problem**: In addition to understanding your audience, you must know what problem you are trying to solve. A hardware company sells products for home repairs. A restaurant feeds the community. Without a problem or a need that creates demand for your services or products, your business may struggle to find its footing.

3. **Understand your offerings**: With your audience and problem in mind, consider what you are able to offer. What products are you interested in selling, and how does your expertise match that product? In this stage of the business model, the product is tweaked to adapt to what the market needs and what you're able to provide.

4. **Document your needs**: With your product selected, consider the hurdles your company will face. This includes product-specific challenges as well as operational difficulties. Make sure to document each of these needs to assess whether you are ready to launch in the future.

5. **Find key partners**: Most businesses will leverage other partners in driving company success. For example, a wedding planner may forge relationships with venues, caterers,

florists, and tailors to enhance their offering. For manufacturers, consider who will provide your materials and how critical your relationship with that provider will be.

6. **Set monetization solutions**: A business model isn't complete until it identifies how the company will make money and turn a profit. This includes selecting the strategy or strategies laid out in the business model types section above.

7. **Test your model**: When your full plan is in place, perform test surveys or soft launches. Ask how people would feel paying your prices for your services. Offer discounts to new customers in exchange for reviews and feedback. You can always adjust your business model, but you should always consider leveraging direct feedback from the market when doing so.

Criticism of Business Models

Joan Magretta, the former editor of the Harvard Business Review, suggests there are two critical factors in sizing up business models. When business models don't work, she states, it's because the story doesn't make sense and/or the numbers just don't add up to profits.

Complicated business models can put off investors and hinder a company's growth. People are less eager to invest in a company they don't understand. Moreover, some business models can be less profitable and at risk of being compromised. What works one year, isn't guaranteed to continue doing so in the future.

Take the airline industry. For years, major carriers such as American Airlines, Delta, and Continental built their businesses around a hub-and-spoke structure, in which all flights were routed through a handful of major airports. By ensuring that most seats were filled most of the time, the business model produced big profits.

However, a competing business model arose that made the strength of the major carriers a burden. Carriers like Southwest and JetBlue shuttled planes between smaller airports at a lower cost. They avoided some of the operational inefficiencies of the hub-and-spoke model while forcing labor costs down. That allowed them to cut prices, increasing demand for short flights between cities.

As these newer competitors drew more customers away, the old carriers were left to support their large, extended networks with fewer passengers.

Example of Business Models

Consider the vast portfolio of Microsoft. Over the past several decades, the company has expanded its product line across digital services, software, gaming, and more. Various business models, all within Microsoft, include but are not limited to:

- **Productivity and business processes**: Microsoft offers subscriptions to Office products and LinkedIn. These subscriptions may be based on product usage (i.e. the amount of data being uploaded to SharePoint).
- **Intelligent cloud**: Microsoft offers server products and cloud services for a subscription.
- **Personal computing**: Microsoft sells the Windows operating system as well as physically manufactured products such as Surface, PC components, and Xbox hardware. Residual Xbox sales include content, services, subscriptions, royalties, and advertising revenue.

3.2 Technology-based Disruptions

Disruptive technology is an innovation that significantly alters the way that consumers, industries, or businesses operate. A disruptive technology sweeps away the systems or habits it replaces because it has attributes that are recognizably superior. Recent disruptive technology examples include e-commerce, online news sites, ride-sharing apps, and GPS systems. In their own times, the automobile, electricity service, and television were disruptive technologies.

Clayton Christensen introduced the idea of disruptive technologies in a 1995 Harvard Business Review article. Christensen later expanded on the topic in The Innovator's Dilemma, published in 1997. It has since become a buzzword in startup businesses that seek to create a product with mass appeal. Even a startup with limited resources can aim at technology disruption by inventing an entirely new way of getting something done. Established companies tend to focus on what they do best and pursue incremental improvements rather than revolutionary changes. They cater to their largest and most demanding customers.

This provides an opening for disruptive businesses to target overlooked customer segments and gain an industry presence. Established companies often lack the flexibility to adapt quickly to new threats. That allows disruptors to move upstream over time and cannibalize more customer segments. Disruptive technologies are difficult to prepare for because they can appear suddenly.

Some of the causes of the emergence of technological disruption are as follows.

1. Development of Digital Technology: Revolution 4.0

Digital technology is developing very rapidly and its distribution has expanded to all corners of the city.

Evidence of its development is the availability of an internet network that reaches all corners of the country. The presence of the internet network makes it easy for users to get and share information in real-time and unlimited. This technological development was later known as the 4.0 revolution.

Another sign of this revolution is the skyrocketing integration and interconnectivity where all ecosystems are becoming more and more connected. For example, the skyrocketing use of IoT or the Internet of Things, information system connectivity, and the emergence of various AI or artificial intelligence-based technologies.

2. The new business model

The emergence of new businesses that have a strong foundation with a technology base also brings major changes to market operations.

These newcomer businessmen develop innovations and improve human resources so that they are able to shift the position of the existing business. For business models that are not ready to transform, they are prone to lose competitiveness.

3. Community Behavior

The development of digital technology is intended to facilitate all human activities and because of that convenience ultimately changes human behavior. Previously, all activities related to physical activity, now shopping or other activities can be done through the palm of the hand.

On the other hand, this change in behavior causes people to have two lives, namely real life and the digital world. And both are flexibly constantly changing and these changes are hard to predict.

As a result, these changes are capable of producing technological disruption.

The Keys to Technological Disruption

The three disruptive technologies that are the key to technological disruption are as follows.

1. Software

One of the keys to technology disruption is software. Application or software development is closely related to changes in companies that are transforming to digital systems.

Especially now that data that was previously in physical form must enter the cloud in large and complex quantities, of course it will be difficult to process if there are no modules that utilize software.

Changes in the company's operations from conventional to modern with this software and can embrace customers in new ways, develop services and products to be more innovative and up-to-date, and increase customer satisfaction.

2. Automation

The second key to technology disruption is automation. In addition to convenience, the key to the digital era is speed. Business in this era is very competitive and operational processes are required to be carried out quickly.

Therefore, you need an automation team and its tools to support business development with satisfactory results.

In fact, nowadays many companies practice automation to cope with a number of workloads. As a result, companies can invest in improving the competence and quality of human resources so that output is optimal.

3. DevOps

Technology has successfully changed consumer behavior. As a result, companies are affected by developing and changing their operations.

The development team is required to bring new breakthroughs and fast updates. At the same time, companies must continue to operate in order to provide user experience and achieve their business goals.

Therefore, many enterprises are using DevOps strategies to accelerate product or output launches and improve user experience and productivity as well as collaboration between teams.

Steps to Face Tech Disruption

Business owners definitely want an agile business, which can adapt to the times and is also successful in its business. Even so, keep in mind that digital will not be able to replace brand image, trust, and service quality. For that, some steps you can take to deal with the era of technological disruption are the following.

1. Human Resources Transformation

HR or human resources is the main asset for a company or organization. Employees who have good integrity and competence, and are easy to master new technology developments will bring the company an advantage over competitors.

For this reason, one way to improve the quality of human resources as a step to deal with technological disruption is by transforming culture to change culture and mindset, as well as increasing the digital capabilities of human resources. This is the main foundation for the digital transformation carried out by BRI to develop this banking giant to be more agile and adaptable in digital adoption.

2. Digital Transformation

Start adapting relevant technologies to support business operations. One of the challenges of the era of technological disruption is the rapid emergence of game-changer tech.

BRI's way to always be able to keep up with technological developments is to ensure that digital talent specializes in this field, looks for relevant use cases in banking, creates innovations that can lift BRI's market segment, and disseminates it throughout the BRI network.

For example, BRI developed BRIAPI as an open banking technology that can improve the effectiveness and transaction experience for businesses. This encourages integration and shaping which in technological disruption is key. In addition, BRIAPI technology is also able to streamline the costs incurred both for businesses and for BRI to be able to be connected to each other.

3. Improved Service Quality and Cybersecurity

The third step in dealing with technology disruption is cybersecurity. Digital transformation has made it easier for various entities and ecosystems to be more integrated, especially in the era of open banking. Thus, further increasing the exposure to personal data as a result of various data processing and exchanges that occur in it. This certainly increases the risk of cybersecurity and fraud as a result of the high traffic.

For this reason, in adopting technology, it is also necessary to prepare a framework that is able to protect consumer and business data, especially personal identifiable information (PII). For example, by meeting international standards for data security, establishing a security perimeter, activating the role of CISO, and cross-sector collaboration to build security.

Examples of Technology Disruption

Artificial Intelligence: One example of technological disruption is Artificial intelligence (AI), which is a digital mechanism created to be able to resemble human intelligence, especially to complete simple tasks. AI is able to search, collect data in the cloud, store, process, and display data carefully. Based on processing and analysis, AI is also able to assist the process of problem solving, formulation, which helps make decisions and answer problems.

Augmented & Virtual Reality: Furthermore, there are technologies that have special abilities to present virtual and additional reality in 3D called augmented reality and virtual reality. With this excellent feature, people are helped when they need to imagine something and determine what they need easily.

Robotics Robotic Process Automation (RPA): This era of revolution 4.0 also produces sophisticated robotics that is able to automate simple human tasks. Through this technology, the robot is able to operate independently after receiving orders from the owner. Robotic Process Automation or RPA is a technology used to automate business processes.

Cloud Computing: Cloud computing technology is an internet infrastructure system that provides a secure, large capacity, and intelligent storage area for user applications and data. Large industries usually use cloud services so that the data they store is safe and can be quickly accessed.

3.3 Digital Business Models: Platform Models

This extraordinary change has come in the form of the digital revolution, a revolution that some have used to create billion-dollar empires. In record-breaking time, they have harnessed the power of digital platforms to reinvent industry business models to win over new customers and digitally enable people to swap information, assets, opinions, services, content and ideas. And with each development in technology and every innovation come more start-ups, fully funded and eager to use their ideas to test new business models and overturn and disrupt traditional industries and strategies.

It's clear that the world of business, like every other aspect of modern life, is changing quickly, but if a company has a business model that's remained unchanged for decades, how are they going to adapt to thrive in this new digitized world? Start-ups have the luxury of beginning with a blank page (and often a blank cheque), able to create their own business models without legacy systems or staff that need to be reskilled. But for traditional companies, it can be a difficult journey.

We can shed some light on that journey, showing how you can introduce your company to business model reinvention through digital platforms, as well as harnessing their value and the many advantages they bring. All journeys will be different, but what remains the same across all organizations is the need for change, the importance of that change and the risks of doing nothing. Your company's digital future will depend on it.

Companies can learn from digital superpowers such as Amazon, Google and Microsoft about how to speed up the adoption of business model innovation. They drive new revenues and greater value from existing business by diversifying their portfolio of business models to include platforms. Digital has many advantages, not least the ease with which products can be added and combined to provide a broader solution that's far better at meeting customer needs and growing revenues than existing alternatives. Digital experience is a crucial part of the way the new digital solution is discovered, evaluated, accessed and consumed, whilst richer digital data at each point drives deeper customer insights, better decisions, more targeted selling and guides innovation. These new digital business models are all centered on digital platform business models.

Platforms form a marketplace that's very different from the traditional fixed and linear value chains familiar to traditional companies. They generate value by bringing together and connecting the key actors of customers, producers and providers (ecosystem partners), facilitating interactions and transactions in a multi-sided model to create a network effect. Any one actor can play one or multiple roles in any scenario. Today, asset-light platform businesses are perceived by investors as having much more sustainable sources of competitive advantage. Once the network effect starts to drive with volume there are lower costs of sales and operation, but then also negligible costs and cash required to scale. This makes platform-based businesses superbly profitable and allows them to re-invest far more in R&D and new product development. Investors see them as most likely to generate future growth, and this is reflected in much higher market valuations compared to both traditional asset intensive and services businesses. There are many ways it can be an evolution that increases value and changes the relationship with customers.

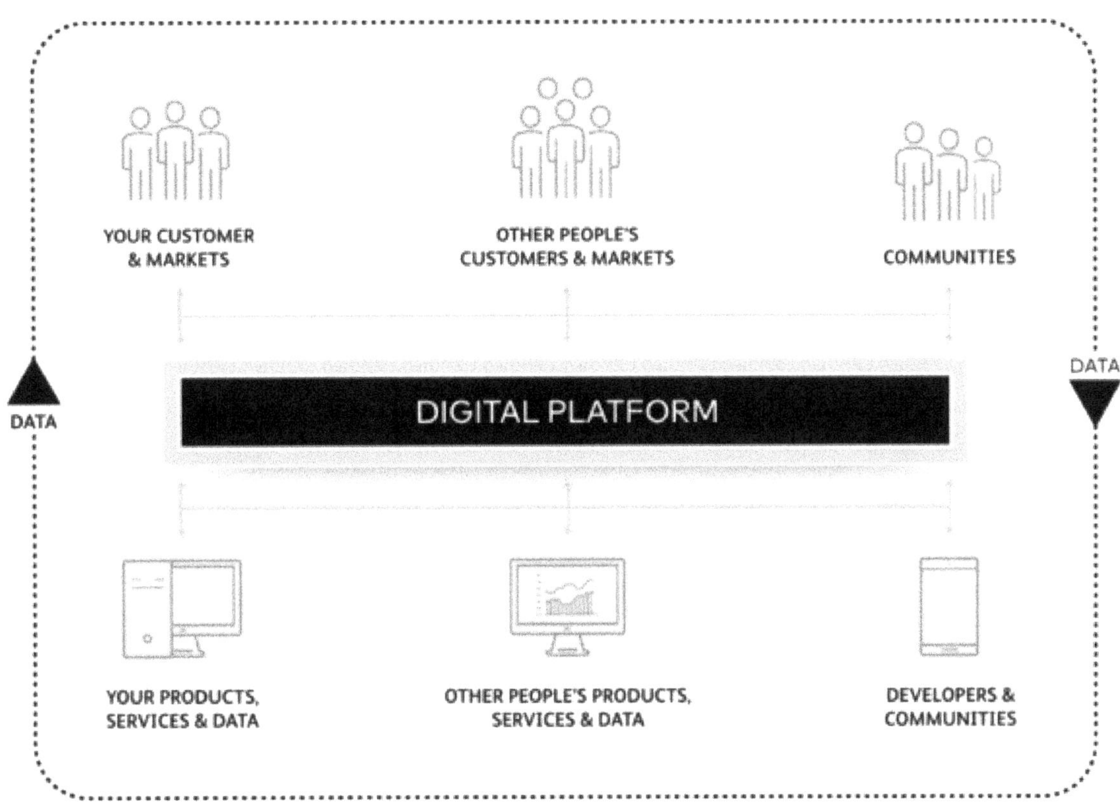

Innovate as fast as your imagination

Incorporating a digital platform model into the current business model requires a clear understanding of the synergies between old and new models. For example, Amazon's acquisition of Whole Foods (ostensibly an asset-based traditional business model) was because Amazon knew it would unlock synergies that Whole Foods' previous owners could not.

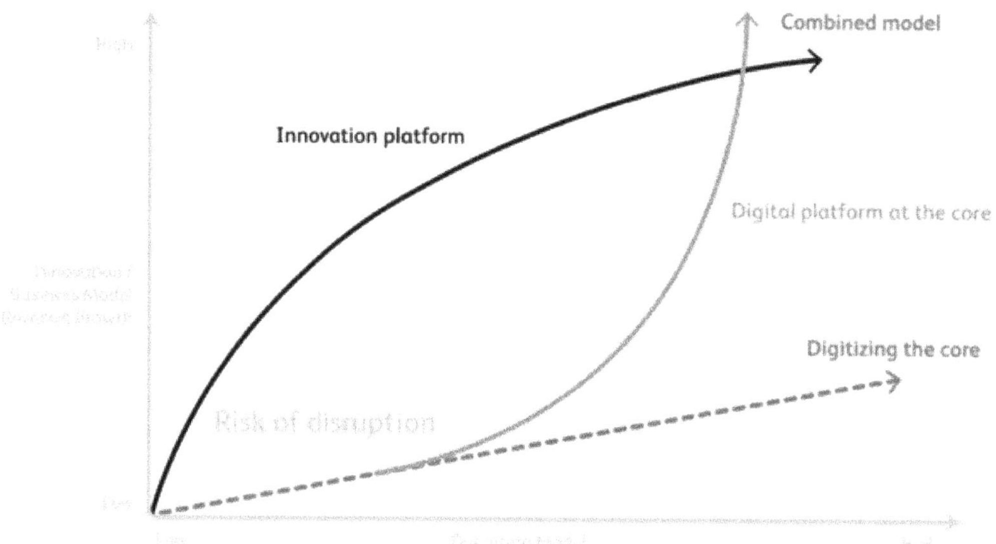

As suggested, there are a number of different pathways companies can take to realise the opportunities offered by the digital platform and unlock the synergies with their existing core business. Each results in a higher level of innovation and revenue growth.

Choosing the right pathway depends on business ambition and priorities, as well as the nature of the competition they face – both existing and emerging. It also depends on how they want to build (and protect) new capabilities whilst aligning stakeholders, skills and culture.

1. Innovation Platform

This stands alongside the existing business and is used to create new digital services and wrappers that can be sold separately. This model is relevant when companies are looking to introduce new digital offerings, embrace new technology or expand into adjacent industries.

The aim here is to use classic digital and lean start-up techniques to innovate and test new digital products to start building a differentiating partner ecosystem that will help with efficiencies and more cost-effectively address customer problems than existing alternatives. The process builds new capabilities and tests new platform-based products. Faster time to market and quick customer feedback are essential ingredients.

Companies facing digital disruption or rapid commoditization of traditional markets often adopt this approach to help re-build their competitive edge. If applied correctly, it gives businesses the advantages of a start-up and the ability to invent ideas: start small and scale up fast when required.

2. Digital Platform at the core

This more evolutionary path starts with digitizing a company's operating model and business processes, reducing internal siloes through the orchestration of several operational environments to provide both immediate efficiency and customer experience gains. This allows the conversion of the core product to be sold as a service linked to specific customer outcomes. It also enables the expansion of core offerings to new digital services through innovation and the ecosystem.

This pathway is an evolutionary change. It is relevant when companies need immediate financial performance gains by improving efficiency, but is also a pathway to revenue growth and a reduced risk of disruption. The model isn't appropriate if there's an immediate threat of digital disruption or a need to radically re-think the business model.

3. Combined model

This is the typical path for digital transformation, which gradually adopts and integrates the two previous pathways. This pathway gives businesses the advantage of innovating fast for adjacent or new digital products that can be added to existing processes to compete quickly with disruption or become the disruptor themselves, while improving efficiency and growth at their core. This is good for thinking about hybrid business models where the innovation pathway is building synergies with the existing core business.

Platform Examples

AirBnB: AirBnB does not own hotels or guest houses, rather it provides an exchange platform on which users can find accommodation or provide access to their accommodation. AirBnB generates revenues by charging a fee for this transaction.

Amazon/Ebay: Do you want to buy a book, golf clubs, a dining room table or even a car. Peer to peer sales platforms such as Amazon, Ebay or Facebook marketplace allow users to sell and buy their goods on the platform. Many of these platforms charge a transaction fee and even provide additional services such as warehousing and distribution of products.

Facebook (Meta): One of the most well known and successful platform businesses, Facebook allows users to share content, view other users profiles, chat with other users, list their business, manage event registrations and much more. Facebook generates revenues from advertising.

Hubspot: Hubspot may have started as a product based software as a service (SaaS) business in 2006 but it is shifting toward a platform model. Rather than limiting their products functionality based on what their engineers could develop, Hubspot opened its doors for other developers to create apps that work alongside Hubspot's core products and now have an extensive marketplace of apps available. By allowing these integrations, Hubspot's users get more functionality and value from Hubspot while some developers charge a fee for use of their app/integration.

Waze: Waze provides mobile navigation assistance but also uses crowdsourcing to allow users to submit their own data and improve the experience for all other users on a similar route. If you are walking or driving and see a road diversion or a car stalled in a lane, you can submit this to Waze who will feed that information to other users in the vicinity. Waze heavily leverages network effects, as more users use the platform, Waze improves the experience for other users thus giving it a competitive advantage over traditional navigation devices.

Types of Platform Business Models

Aggregation platforms: These bring together users and facilitate an exchange of goods, services or information, for example eBay and Etsy. Aggregation platforms tend to be transaction or task-focused. The platform facilitates user transactions and generates revenues via transaction fees or a charge for access to the platform.

Social platforms: Social networking platforms (Facebook, Instagram, Twitter, Youtube etc) aggregate users, but not purely for the goal of transaction. They facilitate user interaction (rather than transaction) and they may generate revenue via advertising. Social platforms tend to foster engagement and relationship building between users in a semi-mediated fashion rather than fully orchestrating the interactions for the purpose of creating transactions. In the case, the social platforms goal is to increase the size and activity of its user base by creating a platform that gives value to users as they use it and encourages them to use it more often.

Mobilisation platforms: These platforms encourage users to collaborate and thus achieve outcomes beyond what an individual could achieve alone. Mobilisation platforms tend to encourage non-transactional long-term relationships among users. These are ideal in a B2B context to foster collaboration among your employees, business partners or even customers to solve challenges. For example, NetFlix wanted to improve the accuracy of its recommendation engine and used crowdsourcing to mobilize individuals/teams from the general public to suggest ways to achieve this.

Learning platforms: Similar to mobilisation platforms, these foster user collaboration and learning over time. For example, Learning Management Systems (LMS) and intranets allow employees to share their knowledge, gain skills, teach each other and learn from your organisation.

Building Your Platform Team

While strategy and technology are important for your platform's success, you must also build an experienced team to manage it. Here are the roles or skillsets needed in a successful platform team.

The Visionary: This person is a strategist who will assess market conditions and the competitive landscape and formulate your platform strategy. They will push forward the strategies implementation with road maps and milestones that are appropriate for both your market and technology situation.

The General: This person is a platform manager will possess multi-disciplinary skills needed for the operations or daily running of the platform. The will be skilled in people management, project management, stakeholder management, finance and have a reasonable technical grounding to be able to collaborate with platform engineers, developers etc.

The Shepard: This person is an ecosystem manager who will establish, manage and grow your external network of partners, developers, users etc who make up your ecosystem. They must be able to be a bridge between your organisations internal strategy and its relationship with the external eco-system who either use your platform or build upon it to contribute to your success.

The Builder: No technology based platform would be possible without engineers to plan, develop and maintain the technical aspects of your platform. Experience into open source systems will be eye. Soft skills are also key as this person will be responsible for working closely with the ecosystem manager and key ecosystem users/contributors to ensure the platform growth is supported.

The Data Whizz: This person is the data manager who will create, maintain and leverage a robust information systems infrastructure in your organisation. It is said that data is the new gold and this person will create and operate your gold mine. They will also install data governance internal into the firm.

The Protector: This person is a privacy and compliance manager who will remain aware of the regulatory landscape and ensure your organisation is compliant. Key compliance areas will include defending against platform misuse by users/contributors, defending against cybercrime/hacking, ensuring user data is secured and helping the eco system manger to build trust among the network.

Traditional product based business models compete on the basis of a static product, functionality, pricing and branding. However, a platform business model allows you to improve your product (if you provide one) and gives your organisation the ability to differentiate itself from product based competitors by providing an additional layer of value to your customers (think of them as users now). We discussed the types of platforms that exist, several examples form some of the worlds most successful platform businesses and they key people you need to develop your own platform business. If you want to learn more about Platform based business or Digital Transformation, feel free to reach out.

3.4 Digital Business Models: Merchant Models

In simple terms, the merchant model is when an online business sources goods from manufacturers and sells them to customers through a webstore. It's a very common online business model and works for an array of B2B and B2C companies, including new businesses and established businesses that want to expand their customer base.

Businesses that use the merchant model don't rely on research and development of their own products, but rather purchasing pre-manufactured products. The business is responsible for website upkeep, branding and marketing, inventory, and secure payment processing.

Many new business owners start with an online-only merchant model, as it is generally simple to set up. The merchant model can work for physical goods that are private label or resells, digital products such as software, or even services - though this is less common.

Over time, however, many merchants may decide to expand by working with resellers, operating brick-and-mortar locations in addition to the online shop, or moving towards a different model of business.

How Does It Work?

1. The first step is to **source products** (or in some cases, services) from manufacturers, wholesalers, or suppliers to later sell them at a markup price to customers. A merchant has to ensure there is enough stock to meet customer demand. When dealing with physical products, a merchant also arranges storage, packaging, and shipping to customers. Some merchants outsource these processes to third parties, use fulfillment services, while others handle it in-house.

2. Another important point is to **work on marketing and brand image**. Merchants often have their own strong brand identity to promote products they sell. But they can also use the manufacturer brand awareness and product recognition to gain customers.

3. After choosing the marketing strategy, a merchant **defines sales channels**. Products are typically sold through various channels, which can include e-commerce websites, mobile apps, marketplaces, physical stores, or a combination of these.

4. Merchants are responsible for **integrating a variety of payment systems with multi-currency support and adjusting secure payment processing** for the convenience of the customers. It involves handling transactions, payment gateways, and financial interactions with customers.

5. Merchants also **provide customer support**: they address inquiries, solve issues, process returns or exchanges.

Advantages of the Merchant Model

The popularity of the merchant model owes to the benefits it offers to the partners:

- **Lower costs**: You will cut down on marketing expenses since the merchant is responsible for advertising and promoting your products.

- **Reduced risks**: As a manufacturer, you will mitigate financial risks associated with the stock management, as the merchant becomes in charge of storing and managing the goods.

Brand exposure: Working with multiple retailers or merchants can enhance your brand visibility. The more places your products are available at, the more recognised your business becomes.

- **Scalability and global reach**: The merchant model allows you to scale your operations both locally and internationally in a more easy and hassle-free way. You can expand your distribution network and reach customers worldwide by partnering with additional retailers without having to invest heavily in the infrastructure or personnel.

Disadvantages of the Merchant Model

Having read about the advantages of the merchant model, you are most certainly ready to contact a retailer. And while the model has the undoubted pros, you also should be aware of its cons:

1. **Intense competition**: E-commerce is a highly competitive space. With a low entry barrier, numerous businesses are competing for the same customer base. This leads to price wars and potentially slim profit margins.

2. **Dependence on Retailers**: You might become dependent on the performance and strategies of your retail partners. If your key retailer faces financial difficulties or operational challenges, it can impact your revenue.

3. **Security risks**: E-commerce sites often become targets for cyberattacks and data breaches. Having a secure payment method will protect you from losing your clients and reputation.

4. **Quality Control Challenges**: If you work with different retailers, maintaining consistent product quality can be challenging, as you have less control over the handling, storage, and presentation of your products.

Merchant Model Examples

Ecommerce Giants

Huge online platforms such as Amazon, AliExpress, Zappos, and Wayfair source products from various brands and sell them online, directly to consumers. Amazon and AliExpress also function as online marketplaces, allowing other online sellers to make use of the merchant model without having to start a website of their own.

Click-and-Mortar

Another example of the merchant model is a click-and-mortar seller. These are brands that have brick-and-mortar stores (sometimes in many locations), but also operate online stores to reach a wider customer base. Examples of these include Best Buy, Foot Locker, and OfficeMax.

Bit Vendor

Similar to the ecommerce giants mentioned above, bit vendors offer products curated from a variety of sources. The difference is that bit vendors sell digital products. A prime example of this is the Apple iTunes store. This model is losing popularity, though, with the rise of subscription-based models for software and other digital products.

The Dropshipping Model

The dropshipping model is often compared to the merchant model. While similar in the idea that sellers rely on sourcing goods from manufacturers, **dropshipping-based businesses don't keep physical stock on hand.** Instead, they act purely as the middleman, and rely on manufacturers to send directly to customers.

The Brokerage Model

A brokerage-model business also acts as the middleman, but unlike dropshipping or merchant model, does not source products at all. Instead, it provides an **online marketplace where sellers can connect with buyers**, and charges a commission for each transaction. Some examples are eBay, Amazon, and Etsy.

The Agent Model

The agent model is similar to the merchant model, but it's more popular for services rather than goods. Agent-model businesses work similarly to brokerage-model businesses, **taking a cut of the revenue instead of providing their own services.** This model is common among online travel services like Booking.com, or freelancing marketplaces like Upwork.

The Subscription Model

In subscription-based models, the business provides recurring access to software, products, or services. Unlike the merchant model, **the subscription model is best for items purchased regularly** (HelloFresh, for example), or media platforms where content may constantly change (NYTimes or Hulu, for example).

3.5 Digital Transformation: Implementation Frameworks/Strategies

A digital transformation framework is used to create a repeatable method of diagnosis, strategic planning and implementation, when it comes to repositioning a business in the digital economy.

The framework ensures the Digital Transformation professional has control over the levers when it comes to achieving a transformed state of a business and the focus extends beyond technology.

The framework keeps focus on the things that matter; customer value, market position and competitors, rather than getting distracted by the shiny lights of technology.

Technology can act as an important inspiration. In our experience however, many digital transformations fail even when the technologists deliver. Technology experts usually deliver exactly what has been asked for. It's what was asked for, that's the problem.

Digital Transformation Framework for Customer Insights

Let's face it, the big consulting firms get it easy when it comes to winning consulting business in the digital transformation space. Their brand carries them through most doors and half way up the procurement staircase. Few question their credentials. However, take a closer look at most of their 'digital transformation frameworks' and you'll find they are exactly the same as the old management consulting tools they've used for the past 30 years. Old, subjective, analogue and not designed for the digital age.

Chief Digital Officers as well as smaller consultancy firms have to show much greater insight before business leaders will take them seriously. They need to come up with fresh insights in context with the customer's business.

But how do you get fresh insights before you start consulting?

Data + Frameworks – that's how!

Finding fresh insights is easy when we use digital transformation pitching frameworks and platforms.

You can tell a lot about a business by its digital footprint. Over time a business publishes its value proposition, those that influence their industry produce a very different data footprint to those that passively participate.

Pitch Fresh Customer Insights

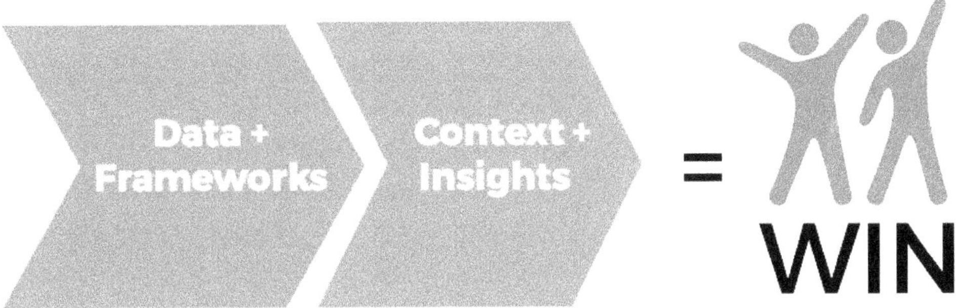

Measuring the digital footprint of a business is very different from looking at its digital marketing. A business can have great digital marketing but a poor digital footprint.

Innovators in all industry and government institutions show similar data characteristics of success over time. The digital innovators outpace those that are just 'doing digital'. These characteristics can be compared against the industry peers and a market position and calculated. This kind of data provides the 'As-Is' state.

This comparison of how a business or business unit is performing against those inside and outside their industry creates stimulating insights and conversations.

Using modern digital transformation consulting platforms and frameworks can be a super-accelerated way of demonstrating competence and maturity in digital transformation. From the get-go you're providing insights even for customers you know little about.

What is A Digital Transformation Framework?

Consider digital transformation framework as a guidebook to achieve smooth foolproof digital transformation with future-proofness.

While digital transformation refers to the integration of digital technologies into various aspects of a business to fundamentally change how the organization operates and delivers value to customers, digital transformation framework refers to a structured approach or methodology that organizations follow to plan, implement, and manage digital transformation initiatives effectively.

In short, digital transformation frameworks provide a roadmap for leveraging digital technologies to drive organizational change, improve processes, enhance customer experiences, and achieve strategic objectives.

There's no universal digital transformation framework you can refer to, as different businesses have their own complexity and need unique solutions. Hence, you need to first understand your business goals and different digital transformation frameworks to find your direction.

Digital Transformation Framework for Strategy

Almost every business gets the term 'strategy' confused with operational plans, targets or even power statements. Many businesses have a web strategy, a social media strategy, a content strategy, a technology strategy, a communications strategy, a HR strategy……Almost all of these 'strategies' are not strategic. They are operational.

Digital transformation strategies use both historic and predictive data to identify new business opportunities. A digital transformation strategy is designed to reposition a business in the digital economy. The repositioning process leverages emerging technology in order to create new products, services and business models that customers favour over the old. Strategies promote rapid exploration, innovation and collaboration. The strategy exposes internal teams to the big 'unknowns' that the company would like solved, linking the deliberate innovation directly with the strategic direction of the business. These strategies are created using digital transformation frameworks.

A digital transformation strategy framework should:

➔ Be purpose built for digital transformation strategy and not a rehash of an old business subjective consulting framework

➔ Consider the entire organisation and how it should change to compete better in the digital economy, not just focus IT functions and enterprise architecture

➔ Platforms, not spreadsheets, should be the tools of the modern digital transformation practice

➔ A modern digital transformation strategy framework should be data-driven to enable data-enriched decision making using predictive-models

➔ The inputs to the frameworks should be dynamic. Actions and tasks should be open to change when new data presents itself

Digital Transformation Frameworks for Operating Models

A digital transformation operating model is organizational design for the digital age. Building a successful business in the digital economy takes different talents, in different roles, doing different things than in the more traditional operating mode.

The operating model describes how a business will leverage the resources at hand in order to meet the strategic needs.

When it comes to digital transformation, especially in mid-to-larger organizations, the operating model will shift depending on the level of urgency when it comes to digital transformation.

From a leadership or consultancy perspective, strategies often fail to show a return on capital when the operating model isn't adjusted to match the strategic ambition.

A simple way to consider which operating model is needed for any given business is to compare the level of urgency for transformation against resources. It's not uncommon that the resources needed don't match the ambition.

Align Business Resources With Strategic Ambition: Strategy >> Operating Model >> Design

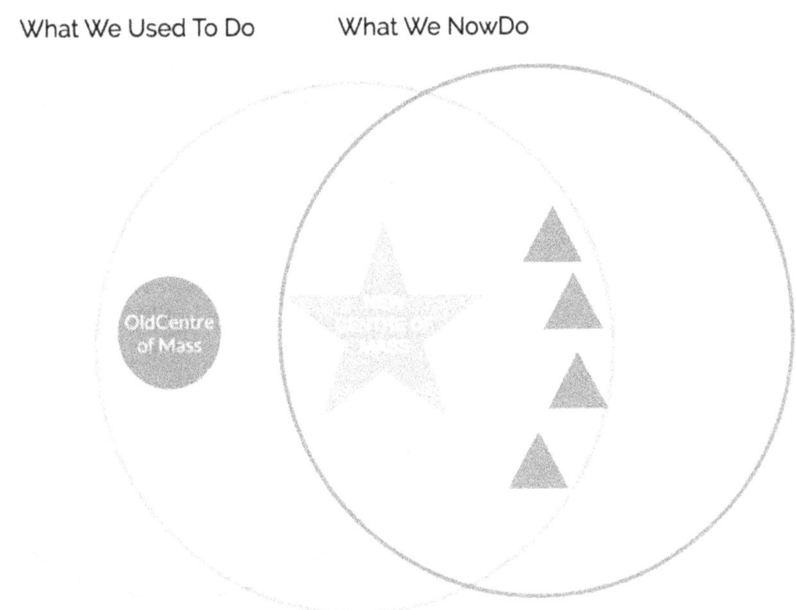

Why Consider a New Operating Model for Digital Transformation?

Businesses that have no immediate disruption on their horizon can choose a different operating model from those that face imminent disruption.

Once the operating model is chosen, only then is it possible to augment the workforce design.

While small businesses often don't need to go to this level of detail, medium to larger businesses most definitely do. In an attempt to maintain 'business-as-usual' and transform at the same time, they underestimate the amount of change required to the workforce in order to achieve their strategic goals.

Too often they assign Digital Transformation to the IT department, give them no authority to change the workforce design or even consider new operating models.

Digital innovators don't face such problems. They use digital transformation frameworks for operating models to help them make the right selection.

Digital Transformation Frameworks for Digital Innovation

Leaders will not be replaced by AI. However, Leaders that understand AI will replace those that don't.

If business units are to leverage the power of emerging technology they must first understand its business capabilities. Digital Transformation Frameworks for Emerging Technologies, associated experiments and learning assets help non-technical leaders integrate emerging technology into their strategic plans.

Too often businesses 'tick the box of emerging tech' by implementing chatbots or IoT sensors in their own offices and factories. They don't have the confidence or the know-how on how to integrate emerging technology into the heart of their strategies and value creation process for their customers.

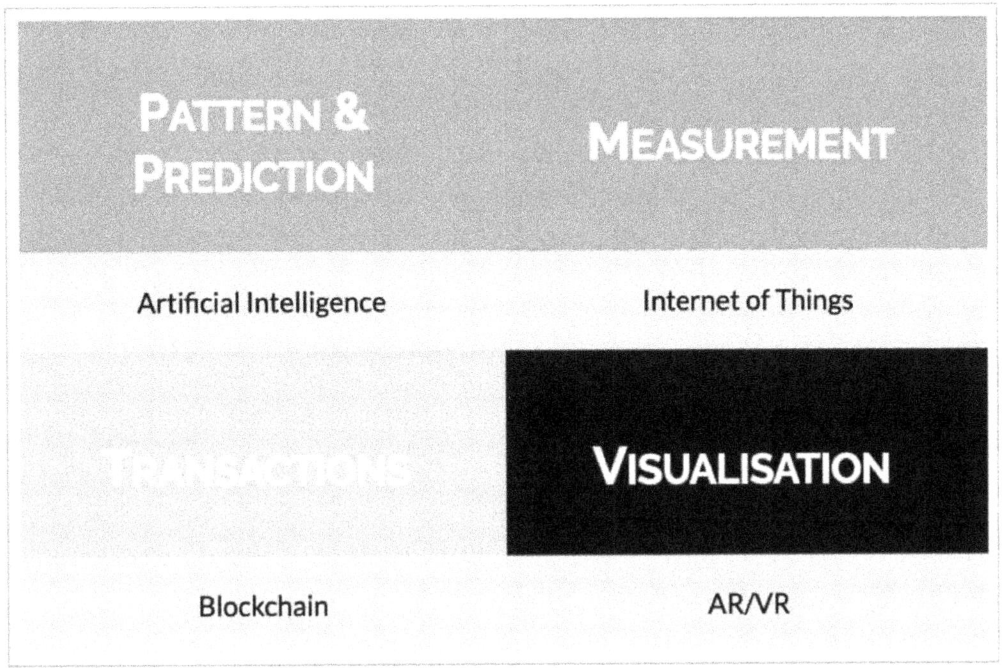

Digital Transformation Frameworks for Emerging Technologies helps bridge the natural gap between technology professionals and business leaders. Technology is an enabler, a tool, it is not strategic in its own right. However, technology can also inspire, guide and help foresee how things will change in the future.

Digital Transformation Frameworks for Emerging Technology such as Machine Learning, Internet of Things, Blockchain and Cloud helps businesses accelerate the implementation of these technologies in order that the business unit can create new, sustained, competitive advantage in the digital economy. Moreover, once business leaders understand the power of this emerging technology it often influences business models and workforce design.

www.ingramcontent.com/pod-product-compliance
Lightning Source LLC
LaVergne TN
LVHW070228170826
845679LV00035B/1874

9798896106319